At the Scent of Water

Nancy Ashcraft

CHRISTIAN LITERATURE CRUSADE
Fort Washington, Pennsylvania 19034

CHRISTIAN LITERATURE CRUSADE

Box 1449, Fort Washington, PA 19034

CONTENTS

ILLUSTRATIONS

"For there is hope for a tree, if it be cut down, that it will sprout again, and that the tender branch thereof will not cease. Though the root thereof wax old in the earth, and the stock thereof die in the ground; yet through the scent of water it will bud, and bring forth boughs like a plant." — Job 14:7-9.

Chapter 1

We Will Not Sow Among Thorns

A date carved on a bamboo tile records that the Karen tribesman Maw Dta was baptized in 1910. By a high stream in the mountains of southeastern Burma, a little group from the church in the village nearby gathered to see him go down into the water. The watchers were Karen tribesmen, but as Christians they had modified their ancient dress to cut out all that had to do with animistic rituals. Adopting the Burmese costume, the women were graceful in long, brightly printed wraparound skirts with blouses and homemade tops of every color. The men, too, wore bright, long skirts, though they were usually checkered, plaid or plain. The company moved, then, as a brilliant splash of color against the green of the jungle growth and the vivid blue of the tropical sky.

The mountains that framed that high, narrow valley were so steep that they seemed to lean, watching, over the group, while fingers of long, silent shadows stretched down from the summits, holding the scene for that moment of time long ago. The dark, flowing stream cast back the reflection of the rainbow clothing, silvery green forest and dark of the silent mountains. But beneath the surface of the water the darting of tiny fish would break up the reflected picture into a swirl of puzzling, meaningless kaleidoscopes. Then, in stillness, the broken picture would settle again to mirror once more the group, the forest, the mountains and the sky.

There was surely a sense of excitement at that baptism, for

one to be baptized, Maw Dta, was a man from that land of spirit worship across the Burma border. In that day and time it was called Siam.

The Christian church in Burma had grown and spread among the Karen tribal people since Adoniram Judson had brought the gospel almost a century earlier. And though the area across the border was peopled by the same tribe, with the same language and customs, the border seemed to act as an impenetrable barrier. There were no Christians to be found among the Karen in Siam.

The colorful band must have chattered excitedly as they moved to the stream, for this was a breakthrough. Maw Dta was marrying a Christian girl and would live for a short time with her family, as was tribal custom. But eventually he would take his bride back to his own land. His baptism, then, would involve this little tribal church in a thrust into the unreached land of Siam across the border.

Karens are a singing people and their song would have echoed up the mountain slopes as Maw Dta made his way down the bank into the stream to meet the waiting pastor, mirrored there in his blood-red homespun jacket. But in that sun-speckled scene of brightness and excited expectation, God alone could see the dark shadow that would grow.

Maw Dta had come in his journeys to this high village. He was weary of trying to communicate with Burmese as he sought by buying and selling and trading to expand the value of a few small items done up in his knapsack. He had been immediately relieved to find that this was a Karen village which welcomed him as one of its own. How good it felt to be called brother, son or nephew after days of being a stranger.

In a world of no roads or hotels, the foot traveler was made welcome in almost every Karen home. The welcome from this Christian community had been so warm that Maw Dta stayed on and on. And for the first time in his thirty years, something began to happen to him.

There was a young girl scarcely half Maw Dta's age. Some think all Karen girls are lovely, with their ivory skin and black hair and dark eyes. Their bodies are tiny, scarcely five feet tall, and they are usually slender and graceful. This girl was all that, and much, much more. To Maw Dta, used to the animist communities of Siam where an unmarried Karen girl would wear only the ancient ritual costume called for at funerals, this girl had broken upon his senses as unbelievably sweet and clean. Instead of a long, loose, dirty sack dress, this child wore lovely wrap-around skirts and soft, long-sleeved blouses. Bathing each evening in the river, she would tuck her skirt of the day under her arms as a bathing sarong and would launder her blouse and that skirt before she left the river.

But it was not so much the cleanness of her clothes that had startled Maw Dta into an amazing awareness of this girl, it was the cleanness of her neck! The slender ivory column that supported the mass of ebony hair in its elaborate braids or rolls was spotless and decorated only by a tiny gold chain. The girls of Maw Dta's hills wore grimy spirit strings tangled with ropes of cheap, swinging beads and costly, but tarnished, gold and silver coins. Because they feared to offend spirits, in times of illness and weariness their bodies and clothes went unwashed for weeks at a time. No wonder the Siamese had nicknamed their Karen "the Yang." For the Yang tree, the rubber tree, was filthy with cuts and slashes to let the dark, sticky sap ooze out to run down into containers. The Siamese, who would later in the century be called the Thai, saw no value or beauty in this dirty hill tribe.

Maw Dta had never thought of his own people as dirty. Not till he saw this girl. And even then he wasn't thinking so much as he was feeling. Maw Dta was in love.

He expected many obstacles to his suit. He came from another country and had no name or reputation here in this foreign land. The jewelry and gems he carried proved he was a person of substance, but only a known reputation would guarantee how he came by that substance. The Christians could read and write and seemed to have knowledge of all the world. To Maw Dta the printed page was a puzzle, and he knew nothing of the world beyond his mountains. Then too, he was painfully aware of his physical shortcomings. The Karen are a small people, but most young men reach five feet and some tower to a good six inches above that mark. Maw Dta was not even five feet tall and he knew he was far from handsome. "Old gopher teeth" he had been called since he was a small boy. There must be a dozen young men in this one village who would be more attractive than he to the girl of his choice, he was sure.

But to his amazement, the girl and her family named only one obstacle to marriage. Maw Dta was not a Christian. He must believe and be baptized. If he would consent to give up animism, the worship of spirits, become a Christian and be baptized, on the very day of his baptism the marriage could take place.

With that story as a background, most Christians would become uneasy about that bright scene by the stream. For what outsider could judge if Maw Dta had truly come to saving faith before he stepped out to meet the pastor and give public testimony to that faith? Yes, the pastor had given instruction to this candidate for baptism. And according to their church structure the elders had interviewed Maw Dta before the day of his baptism. But that day was also to be his wedding day. Maw Dta was in love. He wanted a bride. Didn't Maw Dta have the most compelling of all reasons to make a false profession of faith? Was he speaking the truth when he answered the pastor there in the stream, "Yes, I believe"? Or with him in a muddle-minded state of love, was it not possible to think that baptism, the outward form, was all that was required to make him a Christian?

It would have been so easy for Maw Dta to think baptism was the door and for him to miss altogether a life-changing encounter with the One who said, "I am the Door." It would have been perfectly natural for him to think in terms of changing religion. It certainly required the supernatural intervention of the Holy Spirit for Maw Dta to realize it was a change of life he needed, not just a change of lifestyle or even direction of life. Nothing less than a new life received from the Lord could make

Maw Dta a Christian. Did Maw Dta experience faith? Did he experience what it was to be born again? Or was there a blankness of unbelief in his heart when he stepped out to give testimony to faith? If Maw Dta was not truly testifying to an experience of life-changing faith, then the little bride would follow her husband back into a land where she would be the enemy of all the powers that were worshiped by all around her, even by her own husband.

But almost fifty years later, Maw Dta, a little old man cruelly bent by arthritis, would beg missionaries to come into the blackness of his hills. After a lifetime of being the enemy of the powers that were worshiped, he still bowed only to the God he had received before his baptism.

It was the little bride, the child of a Christian family, the girl so clean and sweet, who carried the seed of darkness. For what she knew in her head she would deny with her life.

When the family moved to Siam they were already growing. Two little girls had been born to the couple. The mother lost her own name, as was Karen custom, when her first child was born. She was to be called Day Zay Moe, mother of Day Zay. But though Maw Dta should have been called Day Zay Bpa, or father of Day Zay — and perhaps was for a time — he was to become so important a person both to the Thai government who gave him the position of headman or representative for his area and to the villagers who chose to live with his leadership that his own name was officially used. By Karen custom he should have been called Day Zay Bpa from the birth of his first child until the birth of his first grandchild, when he would again lose his name and be called Gaw Lay Poo, or grandfather of Gaw Lay. But importance canceled custom and he was called Maw Dta until the day of his death.

In a land where Karen are semi-nomadic, moving every two or three years when they have exhausted the farming potential of the nearby hills they've burned off for planting, Maw Dta established a village that was never to move. Flat rice fields were cultivated and some fruit and flowering trees were planted. That village would bear his name, Maw Dta. But the honor given Maw Dta by the villagers and the government officials seemed a hollow vanity to the man. The honor that would have mattered so much to his peace and comfort was always denied him, for that lovely bride from Burma would always scorn his leadership.

Arriving in Siam, Day Zay Moe threw off all Christian duty. Without a time of family worship, Maw Dta, who could not read, was as an amputated limb that would wither and dry without nourishment. He pleaded with Day Zay Moe to read to him, but she had no desire to hear the Word of the Lord for she had become fascinated by the occult practices all about her. She had listened to the spirit doctors chanting to the spirit of the wind, the spirit of the fire, the spirit of the water and the spirit of the earth. She had watched them draw their signs of power around the bodies of the ill and the homes of the troubled. She tasted medicines gathered from the forests at the full of the moon and blessed by ancient unknown gods of darkness.

Listening, watching, tasting, she was drawn. And at last she was ensnared.

Day Zay Moe knew the Word of God would sound as an alarm, annoying her conscience as she moved into the darkness. Her studies of rules, of legends, of chants, of potions and charms involved a deep commitment and she had no time to think of the Lord. In time she became famous for her power as a spirit doctor. Power to read the future and tell fortunes, power to diagnose illness and prescribe cures, power to cast spells and to charm was hers. Maw Dta was appalled at the way she had chosen. But anything he would say was met with mockery and the humiliating rejoinder, "You know nothing of your religion while I have become renowned as a doctor of mine."

With the putting away of family worship and personal worship had come other changes in Day Zay Moe. Although she remained an immaculately clean woman, she was seldom sober as afternoon wore into evening. Her family grew up with the aroma of their mother's still brewing whiskey at the back of their house. In the evenings when she was far gone in drink, they would hear her sing hymn after hymn, all interspersed with bawdy songs and the chants of spirit worship.

Up above the bamboo slats laid across the rafters of their house were two bundles wrapped in oilcloth. One was Day Zay Moe's old Bible and hymnbook. This bundle was seldom moved. But the second bundle was taken down almost every day. It was raw opium brought down from the high hills by a Meo tribesman. Day Zay Moe bought a supply from him several times a year and resold it bit by bit at great profit. Maw Dta had found and destroyed the bundle more than once. But Day Zay Moe became clever at hiding it, first in their home and later in the homes of their married daughters. Heathen Karen called Day Zay Moe "the Christian spirit doctor" and "the Christian opium seller." Maw Dta thought his shame could surely never be greater.

When Day Zay and Do No, a younger sister, reached school age they were sent back to Burma to attend a Christian school Day Zay Moe had attended as a girl. Perhaps it was a matter of pride before an illiterate heathen community and her relatives across the border that prompted Day Zay Moe to take this step that might have undermined her life as a spirit doctor. But what was Maw Dta's motive? Did he hope his daughters would return from their schooling so soundly converted that they would be able to stand against their mother's influence? Did he hope they would teach him and the rest of the family the secrets hidden in the Book he could not read? The motives and desires of long ago are hidden, but the results remain to be studied. The two girls eventually returned from Christian schooling to become spirit doctors as had their mother before them.

Then came a time when Maw Dta and several other men of the village were away logging with their elephants in an area far to the north, near where Siam was hemmed in by Burma and a portion of French Indochina, later to become Laos. It was over a year before the job was finished and the men, who had not heard one bit of news from home, could at last return. Maw

Dta was met with the news that his wife of twenty-five years was just ready to give birth to a baby. There is no record of the shock and anger that Maw Dta must have felt. His grief and shame at being betrayed by his wife remain concealed.

When anger is controlled and disappointment contained, a man appears unemotional, unfeeling, uncaring. The code of heathen Karen demanded that a man be in such control of himself. The honor given to Maw Dta over the years proves that he was in such control of himself. He stood the test. Whatever he truly felt could be seen by no one.

Though Maw Dta's sense of betrayal was private and hidden, we know that from that time on Maw Dta slept in the homes of his married children, one after the other, and would never again live in the house with Day Zay Moe. He would support her financially and care for her in illness, but in the truest sense he had divorced her.

Was Day Zay Moe now being called by her heathen neighbors "the Christian adulteress"? Before the spirit-worshiping Karen this was the one and only picture they could see of what it was to be a Christian. And the darkness of the testimony would deepen with the changing political scene of those years.

In January of 1948 Britain gave independence to her former colony to become the Union of Burma. But without British authority the tribes — Burmans, Karen, Shan, Kachen, Mon and Arkanese — could not live in union. Before the year was over, the other tribes were at war with the Burmese.

Guerillas of the Karen Liberation Army came seeking out sympathy and supporters across the border in Thailand. It was not long before Day Zay Moe's relatives had found her and her family.

The soldiers who came through the sun-speckled bamboo forest were usually young, for a boy could join the Gaw Thoolie (Karen Army) at age thirteen — and only after ten years could he apply for leave, if he were not discharged before that time, crippled and maimed in body and mind. Their uniform was usually a checkered sarong and rubber sandals. And they were as apt to carry a guitar as a carbine rifle.

Though their dress was unorthodox, the zeal of their war had eaten them up, and far into the night they would spin their stories of strategies for ambush and counter-ambush. Candles set on rusted Ovaltine cans would burn low, flicker, and go out before the boys tired of telling of their exploits in war. Soldiers who came to Maw Dta's village were often Christians. They would tell of their raids on defenseless travelers and merchants and then have a prayer meeting, calling on the help of God in heaven for their war. It was not surprising that the villagers got the idea that this was a Christian war. Often the zealous young soldiers were persuaded of this themselves. Theirs was a holy war and the glory of their victory soon to be won had made them drunk.

Their talk and dream took a compelling hold on some of the young men of Maw Dta. Eventually several would go to war, and two would never return. These two were sons of Maw Dta.

Maw Dta had many daughters, but just two sons. One was killed in ambush. And if there could have been any glory in that fact, it was quickly tarnished by the eyewitness account of others who escaped the Burmese trap. Maw Dta's son had been worse than drunk, for he habitually mixed whiskey with the smoke of the opium pipe. When Day Zay Moe heard of her son's death, did her eyes dart quickly to the bundle in oilcloth hidden up by the rafters under the leaf roof? Did she think of her own whiskey still? Did she at all blame herself and her example? This was the son she had sent so many times to fetch from the rafters the opium she would sell.

The second son died, if anything, in an even more dishonorable way. With soldier friends he had crossed back into Thailand, their almost non-existent soldier's pay long overdue. In their attempt to hold up and rob a household, they were all killed. Word was brought to Maw Dta by government officials; his second son had been killed as a common thief.

Maw Dta knew he was not without blame. He should have learned to read those long years ago as a young bridegroom in Burma. He should have taken on himself the position of teacher in his own home. He was deeply ashamed that, while he was an acknowledged leader among men, he had given no leadership to his own family.

At last, moved by his own sorrow and burden of guilt, he sent word back to the little mountain village that had been home to Day Zay Moe as a child. He begged for the church leaders to send someone to teach him, to teach his family and his village.

"No," came the answer. The Thai hills were famous, or infamous, as a place of robbery, of opium addiction, of murder. No one would come. In the poetic language of the hills, the church sent word that they would "not sow among thorns." Maw Dta did not look at the hills, he looked at himself and his own family, and he knew he deserved the reply.

Do not harshly judge the little Christian community in Burma. They knew that their denomination had supported a missionary to Siam, now Thailand, for almost forty years — a lifetime. And he had seen no response to his message. Summer workers had gone from the Bible schools of southern Burma and had returned to report no conversions. The Karen soldiers who visited the village of Maw Dta could tell of the darkness and occult practices, even in Maw Dta's own home. The little Christian community was adopting a stand that thirty years later many mission societies and conferences would accept. Work among the *responsive*. Do not waste personnel and funds among the unresponsive. Great mission societies would make it a policy not to sow among thorns.

But this is a horizontal picture of missions, where men pick and choose and refuse. There is a vertical picture of missions, for the Lord of heaven is still the Lord of the harvest on earth, and He is the One who sends forth laborers into His harvest fields. Would the Lord of heaven refuse Maw Dta because of the darkness of the situation? Would heaven's pronouncement concerning Maw Dta and his hills be the refusal, "We will not sow among thorns"?

Chapter 2

A Village of the Uncounted

Early in the decade of the fifties, a small band of missionaries to Thailand trekked through the hills bordering Burma. It was a survey trip to find and number the unreached Thai villages hidden back in those rugged hills. No one knew who was there. The border range was unmapped and its people uncounted. The missionaries working among the Thai of the great riverside cities could not escape from that silent presence of blue mountains stretching as far as the eye could see from north to south. At last, laying aside their pressing jobs, they went off to find out who was hidden there in the mountain folds. The missionaries planned to have evangelistic meetings, and if they found anyone who could read they would give out tracts and gospel portions.

One evening their walking brought them to a few bamboo huts beside a mountain stream. Here the people seemed oddly indifferent to them. There were no calls of greeting or welcome as the missionaries entered the clearing of the village. Only the small children reacted to the huge white strangers who had suddenly come out of the shady jungle forest into the brightness of the village clearing. With squeals of fright they scattered quickly and disappeared into their bamboo houses. To the greetings of the missionaries, the adult villagers made no response at all. What was this? A village of the deaf?

The villagers might all have been deaf for all the Thai that they could understand. Only when the village headman was summoned were the missionaries brought to understand that this was a Karen tribal village. Even the little old headman's understanding of the Thai language was so limited he could not grasp the purpose of this visit from foreigners. The tiny Karen man seemed worried and distrustful, but his catching sight of the cross on a booklet held by one of the missionaries worked a sudden, dramatic change. A gopher-toothed smile amazingly transformed this solemn headman. He beamed with joy — and in a flood of Karen mixed with snatches of northern Thai, with many handshakes and hugs he brought the bewildered missionaries to understand that he was a believer, a believer who had waited forty years for a missionary of the cross to come to his village.

Seated on the floor around a low, round table heavy with steaming plates of rice, the missionaries tried to sort out the story they had heard in such garbled language. Maw Dta, the headman, had come from Burma more than forty years before. And all these others, women and children of all ages and sizes that crowded the room behind them, who were they? Were they related to Maw Dta and were they Christians too? No, surely not, for there were spirit strings about most wrists and necks. The women's teeth were blackened by the constant chewing of the betel nut and the bamboo floor was stained where the blood-red juice had been carelessly spat. Even tiny children puffed away on long, silver tobacco pipes.

Later in the evening, when Maw Dta organized a meeting, the group with spirit strings, silver pipes and betel nut-stained teeth joined in the singing of gospel hymns, singing with great gusto, and by heart, song after song. The words were all strange, but the tunes were long-loved friends, and so the missionaries joined in in their own language.

Maw Dta then shared with the missionaries the heavy burden of his heart. His family and his own Karen people were dying without Christ. Here, surrounded by the darkness of spirit worship, he was losing his family, one after another. He could not read and the lessons he had learned long ago had been told and retold. The sons, he knew, had been faithfully taught, but still not one of his children had come to receive Maw Dta's God. His family would sing the songs he taught, but they did not believe the message of those songs. And behind him, lost in the hills, waited village after village where the gospel had never been preached.

One of that little band of missionaries was Wilfred Overgaard, a brawny young American. Wilf had been serving in Thailand for three years, having arrived shortly after the Japanese occupation forces had departed, and was now field leader for the Worldwide Evangelization Crusade, with ten workers in the country. As Wilf listened to the broken Thai of Maw Dta, in his heart that voice took on the accents of the highest command. And the Karen became a part of the vision and challenge of the WEC mission in Thailand. Maw Dta's burden had become WEC's orders.

But Maw Dta's years of waiting were not yet ended. The WEC functioned in Thailand as a fellowship of missionaries. Though Wilf Overgaard had been unanimously elected field leader, his authority as leader did not extend to the arbitrary placement of personnel. Wilf might encourage likely new recruits to consider work among the Karen, but with such encouragement his authority ended. Wilf would have to wait with Maw Dta to see the Lord of the harvest direct workers to those unevangelized hills.

Would Maw Dta yet again be refused? He had at first hoped Wilf and his wife Evy would come and work among his people. He recognized Wilf as a leader and had hopes that the very weight of Wilf's personality would influence his people to consider the claims of the God of creation. One can imagine how he must have brooded as weeks stretched into months and finally into years, and no one came to answer his plea.

Wilf knew that the Lord was not leading him away from the Thai work that so claimed all that he had to give. But he felt that God would have him open a station where missionary recruits could study the Karen language. And this he did.

Wilf and Evy rented a house in the little border town of Maesod. The town is separated from central Thailand by high mountain ranges. As is true of most Thai towns along the Burma border, the site had once been a tiny Karen village. But as drought and famine years had driven more and more Thai families across the mountains to settle in the fertile valley by the border river, the Karen had moved out, retreating further and further into the hills simply because they did not choose to mix with any other society or culture. The Karen name for themselves in their own language is a word meaning "human"; they consider all other groups and nationalities as slightly less than human.

Though there were none of the mountain Karen of Thailand remaining in Maesod, the guerrilla warfare across the border had driven some of the Karen of Burma to flee for refuge to the little border town. These were not only Christian Karen but highly educated Karen, speaking the English of a British school system. Wilf saw them as potential language teachers for the missionaries who would answer Maw Dta's call.

With excitement Wilf watched the language progress of two missionaries, Bob and Alice Peters. This young couple had come from America, engaged to be married and committed to a life of pioneer evangelism. Bob and Alice were not dismayed at the picture of life beyond reach of roads or electricity or running water. They were not asking for a comfortable or easy life, but rather for a life-consuming vision. The idea of trekking through the hills to unreached villages was a vision worthy of their lives, and they did not count their strength or health as precious commodities to be guarded. That God had called Bob and Alice to work among the Karen seemed so very suitable.

Completing a course of study in the Thai language, Bob and Alice moved on to Maesod to study Karen with the refugee teachers Wilf had lined up. Quickly they found themselves identifying with this scattered people, without land or government. The urgency of the task before them drove them on in a relentless concentration of study. Soon the language would be theirs, and Maw Dta's request would be answered.

Nearing the end of the time they would give to formal,

full-time language study, the Peterses went on a survey trip through the unmapped hills. The inhabitants of each tiny settlement of straggling bamboo houses would tell them how to reach the next village. It was unscientific. They probably missed as many villages as they visited. But their trip translated the job before them from just a vision into flesh-and-blood reality.

People
   People
      People

Faces and names and stories filled their minds. Strangely, the settled assurance came. God was not leading them to Maw Dta's village, but a village in quite a different direction from Maesod began to fill their thoughts. Wilf could hardly believe it, for Maw Dta's invitation seemed to Wilf to be the obvious door of entry to the closed Karen hills of the border range. But Bob and Alice were certain that Maw Dta was not the door God was opening for them.

Bob and Alice had already moved to a Karen village several days' journey from Maw Dta when I was introduced to Maw Dta and the Karen. As a new arrival in Thailand I had heard the story of the little old headman who had waited a lifetime for the messengers of the cross to come to his people. On one level I longed to be the answer to Maw Dta's heart cry, but on a more practical level I felt so completely unsuited for such a work! Thai language study was showing me that I was certainly no linguist. If God was stirring my heart to answer Maw Dta's request, then I would have to undertake yet another language. And I would never choose myself to be a pioneer missionary among an unreached people. I am certainly not brave or particularly aggressive.

The idea that God was calling me to spearhead an attack on a satanic stronghold left me dumbfounded. Surely I was better suited to follow up such a move! On the physical level, even in the ideal climate of California, I had never been athletic or energetic. In the steamy heat of Thailand's rain forests I found I had all the energy of a noodle floating in boiling soup.

Wilf was not particularly excited when I told him that I felt called to the Karen. I had come to Thailand at twenty-two years of age, just out of Biola Bible College. Wilf knew that a single woman who still looked like a coed was hardly what Maw Dta was requesting.

Bob was not especially encouraging either. One of his first remarks when he heard I had been called to Karen work was, "We must be molded into a team." How sinister I thought that sounded, since he and Alice were already a team. Guess who needed the molding!

Maw Dta had been told that the Peterses were studying Karen and so he had adjusted his expectations from Wilf to the Peterses, but without enthusiasm. Bob and Alice were newlyweds without children. Young married Karen who have not proven themselves are never recognized as leaders in a village community. A man must prove himself — show ability in farming and building, planning for and supporting his growing family. Many men fail and turn to opium or drink to forget their inadequacy. Few survive the tests to be accepted as mature elders of a village.

Maw Dta had not been given a choice, but he expected this young, untried couple to come to his village. And because of his invitation, Maw Dta would have to be responsible for them. If Maw Dta felt uncomfortable about the immaturity of a young married couple, then how would he feel about a single girl coming as a teacher to his village?

Wilf, in a last effort to influence the Peterses to consider Maw Dta's invitation, organized a jeep trip to the headman's village. This was 1958, one of the few years when a temporary road was opened into that area by the lumber companies for their huge logging trucks. The road, though little better than a track deep with red dust, cut through the jungle all the way from Maesod to Maw Dta. This was a luxury we missionaries would not experience again for many years.

The Peterses were willing to be a part of this trip, but their subsequent refusal to accept Maw Dta's request was so emphatic that Wilf had no other choice than to include me in a second trip. Wilf would expose me now to Maw Dta, his personality and the need of his people. I knew that I should never have been included in such a trip at that stage of just beginning the Karen language except that Wilf, making an effort to accept the Peterses' refusal, now gave me the chance to consider if Maw Dta's village was the Lord's choice for me. But I knew that Wilf still hoped that Bob and Alice's refusal was not final. He longed that they might find that the Lord was leading them to the headman's village.

I began almost immediately to hope that Bob and Alice would not change their minds. There was nothing in the natural circumstances that can explain that desire. Even by jeep, the trip was long and hard, and very hot and uncomfortable. What would it be like to walk those weary miles?

The village was just a group of something like fifty moldy bamboo huts, without even the most meager comforts or any standard of sanitation. The running water was the river, and if I felt that my bath in that river was really making me clean, I was cured of that silly idea when I glanced over my shoulder and saw a family of pigs crossing just upstream from me. But I knew the hardest thing about living in Maw Dta would be the food problem. Maesod, twenty miles away, was the closest market, and for most of the year there would be no road at all covering any part of those twenty miles.

I can only explain that my desire to be a part of the answer to Maw Dta's call for missionary teachers was a rising excitement that God was so leading. I had just completed my study of the Thai language and I would need at least a year in Maesod to study Karen. I knew there probably would be an even longer delay before I could move to Maw Dta, for I had no co-worker. The WEC fellowship of missionaries would surely feel that I ought not to make such a move without a co-worker, for it is mission policy to send out workers at least by twos into unevangelized territory. I would have to wait until I had a companion.

I was very much taken up with my own view of that trip to Maw Dta; it was discouraging to think of the months, perhaps years, that stretched ahead before I could even begin to answer the headman's request. Had I been able to see that trip from the Karen viewpoint, however, I would have been horrified.

Mu Lay Bpa, married to Maw Dta's second daughter, would one day years later tell me just how offensive that invasion by foreigners had been. The jeepload of missionaries had arrived to be welcomed at grandfather Maw Dta's house. With just a temporary logging road making the village accessible to the outside world for a few weeks every five or six years, this arrival of a jeep was an occasion of tremendous significance. Most of the villagers had never seen a jeep before, and only a few of the men had ever seen a Westerner. It was thought to be only right that Maw Dta, as headman of the village, should be the one to receive such guests. And it was known that the leader of the group had been a friend of Maw Dta for several years.

Word spread quickly that there would be a meeting in the evening. Mu Lay Bpa, now bathed and dressed in his best clothes, waited to be summoned. He was Maw Dta's son-in-law. He owned fields and livestock and an oxcart. He was a man of substance and importance. But his greatest claim to honor was that both he and his wife were spirit doctors. There were no more than two or three men in the village who could expect as much honor as Mu Lay Bpa could take for granted. While he waited for the invitation that would give him the honor due him, a great roaring pressure lantern suddenly glared out into the velvety darkness. Then, to his dismay, a hideous loudspeaker began to blare away, shattering the peace of the evening. The crowning offense was that the blaring noise was in Thai. "Do these ignorant foreigners not know that they are in a Karen village?" grumbled the frustrated Mu Lay Bpa. He was so disturbed that his status in the village had not been recognized with a personal invitation that *everything* about the meeting irritated him. Mu Lay Bpa would speak years later of that horrible loudspeaker. "It was more annoying than the buzz of mosquitos, and more painful than the squealing whistle of locusts."

Though the teaching of the evening was translated into Karen, it was an added insult that the translator was a widow whom everyone knew was a renegade, for she had betrayed her people by marrying a Thai. Massey was well known in the hills. She was a daughter of a national missionary from Burma who had lived in Maesod for forty years without winning any converts, not even his own daughter. Massey had been sent back to Burma, to the same Christian school attended by Mu Lay Bpa's wife Do No and his sister-in-law Day Zay. Massey, too, had returned to Thailand to deny the faith taught in that school. This, of course, would not have prejudiced Mu Lay Bpa or any other Karen against her. Rather, it was the fact that she had turned from her own culture and married a Thai that caused the Karen to think of this woman as a renegade.

Mu Lay Bpa sat, then, in offended dignity in his darkened home that night. With his ears he could not escape the din of the loudspeakers which went on and on. But his mind turned off and never received anything of the message that was given. In fact, none of the important men of the village attended the gospel meeting, for they had not been honored by an invitation — a request that would have acknowledged their place of authority in the village. Though none could get away from the preaching, in their offense none heard the message of the words.

The missionaries, except for the Peterses, were all workers among the Thai. They knew nothing about the Karen culture at all but assumed that Maw Dta would advise them about how they should act and as to what would not be acceptable in Karen culture. They did not realize that Maw Dta was in such awe of them as foreign teachers of great importance that he never dared to make any suggestions at all. The poor man must have been most uncomfortable as he became aware that none of the other village leaders had come to that meeting.

This was a faux pas of which Wilf and the other Thai workers would never have been guilty in the Thai culture. Never would they hold public meetings in any area without first visiting the local officials — not only to ask permission to hold their meeting but to give special invitations to those in authority. But they never dreamed that there was a structure of social distinction in that crummy bamboo village, and they never realized the offense they gave by not honoring those in authority.

If Maw Dta had been aware that the Peterses were not interested in his invitation and that another in the group — a girl the same age as Gaw Lay, his own irresponsible grandson — was the one Wilf would count on to fill his request, he probably would have canceled the whole thing.

God had canceled nothing. He was moving for Maw Dta. Mary Lewin, a young lady from England, would shortly announce that she believed it to be the mind of the Lord that she join me in Maesod for Karen study and the eventual goal of entering Maw Dta's village with the gospel.

Our backgrounds were completely different. Mary was from the top drawer of British society. Her clipped accent and distinctive handwriting told the initiated that she had attended one of the finest public girls' schools (a "private school" in American terminology). Her manners and manner were impeccable. I ought to have felt very plebian and uncultured in Mary's presence, but I didn't. In fact, a tremendous weight I hardly knew I carried was suddenly gone with Mary's announcement that she was joining me.

Mary's lively sense of humor made me immediately feel at home with her. There had been times in my short missionary career when I had felt that the lives of missionaries were heavy and without humor. I had thought, "I'll never laugh again." What a relief, then, to have Mary, who could always see the humor in a situation, to be my co-worker!

There was another facet of Mary's personality that I greatly appreciated. Though Mary would always willingly obey the Lord and make any sacrifice that was required in His service, she didn't talk like the heroine of a missionary novel. Mary had no pious affectations at all. While working about the house she was as apt to break into some comedy song from Gilbert and Sullivan as she was to sing a hymn. Mary didn't speak of our

future move to Maw Dta as some "glorious privilege." Instead
she bluntly referred to it as a ghastly prospect which she called
"mud-hutting it."

It was a great relief to me to realize that Mary was not
trying to fit anyone's concept of a spiritual missionary, nor was
she going to try to mold me into any image she had of a
spiritual missionary. We could relax and be ourselves with
each other, and that made it so much easier to get on with the
job and the adjustments ahead of us. Looking back, I realize I
had many changes that needed making. I needed a great deal of
molding. But the adjustments from American school life to the
Thai culture and then to the Karen culture were so demanding,
so drastic, and those changes came so quickly, one after
another! The Lord knew I had all the adjustments I could
handle. I would have broken emotionally under a critically
demanding co-worker.

Though Maw Dta would not have chosen us to evangelize
his village and hills, and we would not have chosen ourselves
for such an isolated and difficult job, God had chosen us. But
first, He would give us a training course of His choosing.

(1) *A typical Karen house and rice barns.*
(2) *Buying meat in the Maesod market.*

Chapter 3

An Open Door to Closed Hearts

The roads of Maesod were unpaved, a soupy red liquid much of the rainy season and a fine red powder in the dry season. The one road over the mountains that connected us with central Thailand allowed trucks and jeeps with four-wheel drive to come westward on even days and to go toward the east on odd days.

There was an airfield just outside of Maesod, and the high point of each week was to watch the mail plane coming down out of the clouds. It seemed that as the plane circled lower and lower for the pilot to get his sighting of the landing field the hundreds of palm trees which shaded the town would brush their fronds against the plane itself. No, Maesod hadn't the most modern of airports. We realized that several times each rainy season — when the men of the town would be called out to dig the plane out of the mud that was the landing strip. In the rainy season of 1959 there were just three resident vehicles in Maesod to convey the townsmen out to the airstrip for this community labor: two privately owned jeeps, and a van owned by the government air company. And when a plane became grounded in the mud the airport van was almost sure to be next to bog down, held by the thick ooze.

There was only one telephone in Maesod, and it was at the post office; from there one could arrange to call any other post office in the country. By so doing your party would be notified ahead of time that he would receive a call from you at such and such a time and would be at his post office ready for your call. Because of the unbelievably bad connection you would have to scream, "Pardon me, I didn't get that" and "Would you repeat that" until you were quite exhausted. But the exciting bit would follow when you had screamed your last goodbye and the line went dead. Every person in the post office and all the closest neighbors would join together, each contributing his version of what he thought the person on the other end of the line was saying. The fact that our conversations were usually with English-speaking missionaries and that our post office helpers knew very little English just added spice to the event.

Maesod had several stores and a fresh food market — a real farmer's market. Every morning at five we would hear the oxcarts rumbling into town, bringing fresh produce for the market: chickens, pigs, ducks and sometimes as many as a dozen different kinds of vegetables, and just as many kinds of fresh fruit. Before noon the market was all sold out; you always knew that nothing was day old in the Maesod market.

Most evenings at twilight the local electric plant would start up and our light bulbs would come on until 10:00. The fact that the generator often broke down taught us to appreciate to the full the wondrous miracle of each glowing bulb.

Yes, the comforts and conveniences of Maesod so many years ago were minimal, but it was a quiet and beautiful town full of the rustle of palm fronds and music of temple bells. If there was ever a traffic jam it was always oxcarts inexpertly driven, whose great wheels could become locked trying to pass each other. Suddenly the helpful town would spring alive to the joy of giving advice, for everyone was an expert in the theory of handling oxen. This town — quiet, isolated from the big events of the modern world — would become the training ground and base camp for our advance into the tribal hills.

How good God was to me there! I happened to be alone in Maesod for one Sunday just before Mary joined me. This was because the missionary who had been ministering in Thai had left that morning on the plane for Bangkok and her furlough. I knew I could expect just one Thai Christian to come for fellowship that morning. I recalled how I had been present months before when this man, Nai Lang, had first come to the mission house. Because of his northern Thai drawl I could then hardly understand him. I had left him seated in our front room while I persuaded Ellen Gillman, a senior worker, to come and talk to him. "He just might be drunk," I warned her. Poor Ellen. She was in the midst of unpacking, for she had just moved to Maesod and really couldn't welcome an interruption just then. But if this were an awkward situation — if the man was drunk — then it was only reasonable that with her superiority in the language she should handle the problem.

In a case of almost progressive shock, Ellen kept adjusting her ideas regarding the visitor. Yes, he was drunk. No, he wasn't drunk — it was his drawling accent that made him appear intoxicated. But whatever, the man was not just another interruption! This stranger wanted to talk about religion, and it was clear from his educated vocabulary that he had studied in the Buddhist priesthood. So Ellen could hardly believe her ears when she realized it was not just a conversation comparing religions that Nai Lang wanted; he was seeking reality and the one thing Buddhism never offered — the forgiveness of sins. And instead of an interruption, that visit became one of the most important hours of a lifetime — for Nai Lang entered into salvation.

In a few weeks Ellen had moved from Maesod and another Thai worker had taken her place. Now, with that worker leaving for furlough and with a shortage of missionary personnel, there was no one to be responsible for the Thai work in that little border town. But Nai Lang had continued faithful and I knew he would come that Sunday morning, expecting fellowship. At first, considering how I should go about ministering to this brother, I thought the obvious way was just to visit with him and in conversation seek to answer his questions and deal with whatever problems he might share. Then I woke up. Who was I trying to kid? As soon as he opened his mouth, I would be lost. Could I answer his questions? — I wouldn't even *understand* his questions! My only chance of being any help to him was to attempt to prepare and deliver a short Bible study. Only the Lord could lead me to deal with the particular topics that touched Nai Lang's life.

When Nai Lang came that Sunday we sat in the front room of our mission house that opened right onto the busy street. This house the mission rented was designed so that the front room could be used as a store: the front wall folded back, opening up the entire room to the street. We sat there in easy chairs in a living-room atmosphere, but even so it was embarrassing to preach to just one person. And it didn't help that Nai Lang, lounging in his bamboo bucket chair, had a thoroughly amused look on his face throughout the entire procedure.

It was all wrong; I could sense it. Nai Lang was old enough to be my father. He had been in the Buddhist priesthood three times and had been held in great respect as a teacher of religion. But the most offensive thing about our situation was not that I was so much younger and of no stature at all as a religious teacher in the eyes of the townspeople, but that I was a woman presuming to teach a man. This was a circumstance dreadfully offensive to the country Thai.

While I was delivering my prepared Bible study I was mindful of every passer-by in the street who stopped to stare at us. But if we had shut the big doors that opened the entire front of our house we could just say goodbye to our reputations forever, for Maesod was waiting expectantly for the inferiority of Christian morality to be revealed. A respected townswoman might get away with visiting a man behind closed doors, but no foreigner representing a strange and distrusted religion could afford such grounds for suspicion. So with those doors open, the awkwardness of the situation was reflected in the faces of everyone who went by in the street.

As Nai Lang opened out his huge black umbrella and hitched up his skirt for the long walk home, I felt sick. We had learned that he came from a village an hour's walk from Maesod. I could not believe that he would ever again make that two-hour trip coming and going, across rice fields, to listen to a girl sputter around in an almost incomprehensible sermon.

All that week I felt physically ill with the thought that Nai Lang would never come again. But then I felt equally ill with the thought "What if he does come?" I could not believe that I had or ever would minister real spiritual life to him. I had explained the situation to Mary, who had now arrived, and she was as overwhelmed as I. We prayed for him, if you can call it prayer when you have neither faith nor hope that what you are requesting will ever be performed. I can only say in my defense that I went ahead and prepared another lesson for Nai Lang. When I didn't feel faith, I went ahead and acted in faith.

The next Sunday Nai Lang came and he did not come alone. He brought his mother-in-law. He had been explaining the gospel for months to his family, and at last this elderly woman had come to faith. Nai Lang brought her now so that I should lead her in a prayer of repentance. She was taking a public stand that she was a believer and follower of Jesus Christ. And was it ever public, with that huge open door!

If my congregation of two was put off by my stumbling around in the lesson that day, there was no sign of it. And they were back the next Sunday with another convert. Each Sunday for the next two years the group grew until there were adults in every chair we owned. By collecting the chairs from every room in the house we had about twenty. Young people were crowded together on benches, on the desk top, and even on the window sill. Smaller children sat on the floor on mats.

The Karen man whose wife had been our language teacher eventually returned to Burma with his family, when the government offered amnesty to Karen rebels. This family gave the Maesod believers a valuable piece of land, and the growing family of Christians set aside part of their weekly offerings with the thought of someday building a meetinghouse.

It would be two exhausting and exciting years before Mary and I had Thai workers to replace us in Maesod and were free to move to Maw Dta. Every lesson took hours to prepare. After our morning's Karen study with the teacher we went straight to the preparation of a Thai message, or we went visiting the Thai believers. All of Wednesday was spent in the small farming village where Nai Lang and most of the believers lived.

This ruined our Karen study. And our Thai vocabulary underwent a change as we developed an amazing repertoire of Thai colloquialisms. Our university-standard Thai was being drowned beneath the idioms and speech patterns of the semi-illiterate Thai with whom we worked.

That we should suddenly have that growing church for which we were responsible before God was a circumstance which only He could have foreseen. That there would be no Thai workers to replace us for two years was something that only He could know or change. But the delay was no mistake. It was an important part of His plan. Those who know most fully what happened in Maesod can never give any credit to human ability, method or goals. God moved when we least expected Him to and we were never prepared to handle the results. To the end of our stay in Maesod we were spectators, watching the Master Missionary at work.

Why had God given us this two-year detour? For us it was an exciting privilege to see Christ at work, seeking out the lost and reaching them in their need and establishing them within a growing church. He gave us lessons to give that formed the new converts into disciples. For us, it was a wonderful experience. But what did it mean to Maw Dta?

We moved by faith, hardly seeing the boundaries of the path we took in moving toward Maw Dta. At that time we did not see that the growing church of Maesod was, in very truth, the open door to Maw Dta. But it was. For otherwise the elders of Maw Dta would have despised their headman for foisting onto them girls who "presumed to be religious teachers." Maw Dta's disgrace at having to champion us might have been the greatest disappointment of his Christian life.

In the two years before we moved to Maw Dta from Maesod we visited the Karen village several times. And men from the Maesod congregation took us in their oxcarts for the various visits. The Karen met Nai Lang, who was obviously a man of importance and property and whose study in the priesthood had set him up as a leader in his community. That he was willing to accept teaching from us caused the Karen leaders to marvel. There was also Nai Promma, who had been a policeman, and his conversation revealed him to be a man of education; in addition, while a Buddhist he had been also a powerful spirit doctor. That he should call Mary and me his teachers stopped any taunts the villagers were ready to throw at Maw Dta. But it was Nai Eye, a man the village had known as a logger, a man who had hired them and their elephants for seasons of work, whose testimony had the most weight. Nai Eye had been looked up to in business dealings. The village did not feel they could now lightly dismiss him as a Christian nor despise us as his teachers.

It was the Christian men of Maesod who paved the way of acceptance for us in Maw Dta, and without them the old headman's position would surely have been painfully uncomfortable. He would have been isolated in his acceptance of us; not another man in the village would have been willing for us to enter their village as teachers of religion.

Yes, Mary and I could not be welcomed with honor by a heathen village but we would now be accepted without ridicule because of the Thai Christians of Maesod. And more important than our acceptance was Maw Dta's position. He did not have to be ashamed of us nor appear before his village as a fool for honoring us as teachers. The delay that established a church in Maesod was a door of blessing for Maw Dta.

The offense of our youth, the offense of our being women — this was something we could do nothing to alter. God first planted a church in Maesod and the Maesod church did much to cancel the offense of who we were. But we would by our own blunders cause additional offense. It was our actions and not who we were that would cause those who would accept us into their village to do so grudgingly and with closed hearts and ears.

A theory once held by some of the great pioneer missions states that new missionaries ought to be completely self-sufficient in going into unevangelized tribes. They ought to be able to build their own homes and support themselves from the jungle. Now it is certainly true that the prescribed one-room structure that all spirit-worshiping Karen lived in would have been most uncomfortable and inconvenient for Mary and me. But it is also true that we knew nothing about building a bamboo house. And so the decision that Bob Peters would serve us by going in first to supervise the building of a house for us was most welcome. We had a basic floor plan in mind, and Bob would make as few compromises of that pattern as he could to oblige us and yet adapt to the ability of the Karen helpers he would hire. It never entered our minds that sending a foreign supervisor to do what the Karen by every right considered themselves experts in doing was a thoughtless insult. We were told years later that not one skilled worker helped with our house. (They really didn't need to tell us that; one look at our new home and we realized no builder was responsible for that!) "Are the foreigners so stupid as to think the Karen don't know how to build bamboo houses?" the offended Karen had muttered.

The theory that missionaries ought to be completely self-sufficient might be a good theory with all other tribes, but in working among the Karen we were eventually to learn that mutual dependence was essential for friendship. Over the years we would help many who would never become our friends; our helping alone was not enough to cement friendship. But we would never receive help from even one who did not give, along with their help, their friendship. And we would have been years ahead in gaining friends among the Karen if we had admitted we needed their help in designing and building our house.

When the time finally came for us to move to Maw Dta, we found that the bamboo for our walls had been improperly cured, and that thousands of tiny bamboo maggots were eating away at our walls. At night we could hear the chomping of their tiny jaws, and the fine dust that covered everything in just an hour or two was explained to us to be our walls being eaten, digested and eliminated by our uninvited guests. Also the slant of our leaf roof was so steep that in parts of our house I could not stand upright.

Bob's hiring the Karen to work under him caused such offense that the Karen gave less than a full day's work and considerably less than their full skill. But there was yet another offense given while Bob supervised the building of our house, and that offense was far more costly than the inconvenience of our poorly constructed house. Years later, Mu Lay Bpa, Maw Dta's son-in-law, would tell us of that second offense.

One day a group of men met on Mu Lay Bpa's front porch. They met to decide what to do about a young man who was a sexual deviate. He had months before molested a small child. A meeting had been called and he was publicly reprimanded, and the village fined him an oxcart load of rice to be paid to the child's parents. The village elders thought surely that would teach him his lesson and that the ugly sin would not be heard of again. But now, months later, a second child had been molested.

As the men talked on Mu Lay Bpa's front porch, seated in a circle, each one sipped from a small pottery bowl of whiskey. They spoke in low voices that could not carry to those who passed by the house. Each one knew what must be done; but how to do it, that was the problem. They knew of no cure for the strange illness that burned in this young man's mind. He must be put to death. For they could all remember from other years and other villages that, as ugly as his sin was, such sin spreads. In the end the final decision was made and a plan was laid. Mu Lay Bpa was chosen to maneuver the young man to his death.

This was not an act of retaliation. No member of the offended child's family had been present at the meeting or would have a part in the execution. This was tribal justice and only the tribal leaders were responsible. When the meeting was over, however, and the men returned to their houses and to work, Mu Lay Bpa was left alone — and such a wave of remorse and bitterness engulfed him that he wanted to cry out his misery to the empty heavens.

The man to be killed, though much younger than he, was Mu Lay Bpa's good friend! How often they had worked together felling trees to clear a field. They had so often set off together into the dark, warm night to hunt in the jungle surrounding the village. The ring of axe on mighty tree would for years bring back to Mu Lay Bpa the ringing laughter of that young man. Never again would he wait in the darkness, sucking comfortably on his old pipe, without hearing in his inner ear of memory the soft voice of his old friend who had so often waited with him for tiger, deer or wild pig.

My Lay Bpa could not excuse the young man's sin. He could not feel that the elders' decision was unjust, but that did not lessen his own pain that a familiar friend would soon be cut off from the earth, and he — he must be one of those administering judgment!

Mu Lay Bpa lifted up his eyes from that circle of whiskey bowls with their silent reminder of the men who had just met and the words they had spoken. Coming out from grandfather Maw Dta's house was the foreigner. Looking back, it seems tragic that Bob, visiting the village to supervise the building of our house, should happen to catch sight of Mu Lay Bpa sitting idly on his porch at that precise point in time. For, not sensing the trauma of the man who always looked so serene and self-confident, Bob wanted to make Mu Lay Bpa realize his need of a Savior. In truth, Mu Lay Bpa was already so overwhelmed by his sense of need that further distress could hardly be endured. And almost against his will Mu Lay Bpa cried out in silence to God, "If there is anything in this man's religion that can draw my heart, I'll break off my spirit strings. I'll tear down my demon altars. I'll destroy every tool I've used as a spirit doctor and I'll become a Christian!"

This was the spontaneous cry of a tortured heart wanting some magnetic force to relieve it of the personal responsibility of decision. I do not know if, in his distress, Mu Lay Bpa could have really heard the gospel. Certainly he did not believe that Bob had any message that would help him. To Bob, climbing the bamboo ladder to the porch, the most obvious thing nearby was a ring of pottery whiskey bowls. Lifting one, he asked, "Have you been drinking?"

That was all that was necessary to send a tortured Mu Lay Bpa into a towering rage. I am sure that his face was controlled, however, and only the note of haughty disdain that he desired to communicate came through as he answered, "I never drink anything stronger than water."

I know just how he looked and sounded, for over the years I have heard his daughter Wa Paw imitate that conversation again and again. With raised eyebrows she would talk down her nose, acting too superior to be offended by the remark, whatever it might be, and would answer with "I never drink anything stronger than water."

This always brought forth a wave of giggles from the other girls, and it was only years later that I was told what conversation she was imitating. Mu Lay Bpa told me the circumstances of the conversation and how he had quickly gotten up from the floor and entered his house to discover several of his daughters smothering giggles at their father's audacity, since everyone knew that he was a dreadful drunkard.

Unfortunately, the offense given added to Mu Lay Bpa's deafness. For years his ears were closed to the gospel and there seemed no way to make him hear. It is probably true that in the agony of that moment in time there was no way the gospel could have been presented that would have broken through his absorption with his own painful situation. I am just sorry that offense was added to offense, for he despised us and went out of his way to avoid us.

When we finally moved into his village there were less than fifty houses there, yet in the two years before we would go on furlough we saw Mu Lay Bpa only half a dozen times. He certainly avoided us. But it was not who we *were* — young, single women, something we could not change — that constituted the greatest offense. It was our decisions and actions, words spoken and attitudes conveyed, that offended most. God opened the door to Maw Dta; we tended to close the ears of Maw Dta.

Chapter 4

The Death of an Illusion

Even the most superficial look at missions reveals that God leads women into areas and responsibilities that are thought to be most suited to men. Certainly God led Mary and me into a village beyond the roads of civilization and the advances of science, and beyond the light of the gospel.

With us to Maw Dta went Massey, who had translated for that first meeting held in the village. Officially, she would be going as our paid servant. Though we could and did share the duties of cooking and cleaning and washing clothes, we could not have done without Massey for long when it came to making charcoal for the cooking, or to carrying water from the river for washing. Then too, because Maw Dta was many hours' walk away from a market, we needed Massey to teach us what forest vegetables could be safely eaten. We would return together from a morning's meeting in a nearby village with our shoulder bags full of ferns, leaves or roots that Massey had pointed out as edible. Then she would teach us how to cook them. How often we wished that she could teach us to *like* them too!

Massey, like all other Karen, was tiny. She was hardly five feet tall. And though she was ten years older than I, and experiences of sorrow and suffering had somewhat deflated her youthful bounce, I could never think of her as an older woman. It was not just her outlook and sense of humor that kept her young, but Massey had two false teeth that were so

35

uncomfortable she often removed them. I never knew whether to expect a sedate smile from a woman in her mid-thirties or an impish grin from a child missing two front teeth.

It was Massey's father who had been sent from a church denomination in Burma to evangelize the Karen of Thailand. But Massey's father had become depressed with the lack of response and the years of no encouragement or Christian fellowship. Back as far as Massey could remember, her father had continued to receive money from Burma for his support, but he had spent most of his time working as a paymaster for the logging companies that worked the huge teak forest of the border ranges.

From earliest memory Massey could recall waiting weeks at a time for her father to return from the logging fields. At last there would come the excitement of the clank of chains in the evening twilight, and a mighty trumpet as an elephant came swaying and snorting up to her parents' Maesod home. In the flash of lantern light her father would appear as if suspended in air, for the elephant he rode was just a bit shorter than the porch. Massey's father would stand and tuck his long skirt up through his legs in a secured diaper effect and then step from his ride onto their porch to be smothered by a "welcome home."

When Massey would talk of her father's return from the logging fields it was obvious that she loved him dearly. But she did not learn to love his God. Growing up, Massey realized her father's faith was real, but she could not help judging the man who received payment for a job as evangelist yet gave all his working time to the job of logging. Her father became wealthy logging, but he lost what would have brought him more satisfaction than money. All his children grew up to judge him and turn from God.

Massey had been sent to a Christian school in Burma, but that was an episode that made no real change in her life at all. It was only when Wilf and Evy Overgaard opened the mission station in Maesod that Massey began to realize the drawing of the Lord. Massey told us how, when the Overgaards hired her to be their servant, she assured them she was a believer. But even as her lips formed the words, her heart reminded her that that was not true. It had been years since she had even thought of the Lord.

Massey had married a Thai man who was a thief and a murderer. At the time the Overgaards hired her, Massey's husband was being sought as an escaped convict. Every crime in the area was blamed on this young man the police were calling "Tiger Yong." Hiding in the jungle, he was expected to strike like a tiger coming upon the unsuspecting in the dark of night. Massey met him each day at a different time in a prearranged place to supply him with food and clean clothing. She knew of the crimes he was committing and felt herself to be a part of them; but she could not betray him. Massey lived constantly with the dread that one day she would hear the news in Maesod that "Tiger Yong" had been killed. She knew that the police would not bother to bring him into jail, because he had already proved that the Maesod jail could not hold him.

The prospect of Yong's death and her partial responsibility for the crimes he was committing while she helped him evade the police became a burden Massey felt she could no longer bear; but neither could she put it down. Her life was miserable. But while meeting with Wilf and Evy Overgaard and the Christian Karen refugees living in Maesod, Massey began to feel the working of the Lord in her heart. Surely this One she had known about for so long a time was now drawing her to know Himself. He was inviting her to commit herself to Him and to trust Him for the salvation she had for so long known only in theory and never in experience.

Massey was experiencing the joy of sins forgiven and peace with God when the news broke in Maesod that "Tiger Yong" had been killed. Massey could only thank the Lord that for several days she had met her husband not only with food and clean clothes, but with a compulsive flow of testimony that she could not restrain. Each day he had listened. For the rest of her life Massey would live with the hope that, like the thief on the cross, Yong had in faith come to know the Lord in that last hour of his life.

To us Massey was so much more than a paid servant. She was a Christian companion and friend. Her longing that her Karen people come to know the salvation of the Lord made her a co-worker. Though Massey was never paid to be an evangelist she did the work of an evangelist — that work her father had forsaken so many years before.

When Massey, Mary and I moved from Maesod to Maw Dta twenty miles away we moved one hundred years back in time. The Karen were offended with us as foreigners. But if the truth be admitted, we were equally offended with their village. Yes, the roads of Maesod were unpaved, but there were no roads at all going into Maw Dta. Even the oxcart trails gave out long before we reached the village. The tired oxen simply carved out a trail as, heaving and groaning, they hauled the carts those last kilometers into the village.

The unpaved airport of Maesod would now claim our great respect, for it was from there that our air mail would come to Maw Dta in the hands of a very tired man who would walk forty miles to and from Maesod, hired by us to carry our mail. The telephone of the Maesod post office would now take its place in our thinking as a rare treasure, for in Maw Dta the villagers didn't know that such a thing as a telephone had ever been invented. The radio could tell us of a crisis in world affairs, but if there was a crisis among our friends or relatives we wouldn't learn of it until weeks later.

But as we had guessed, it was the fresh vegetable market we missed most of all in Maw Dta. "Have you noticed how furry and unpleasant boiled pumpkin leaves are?" asked Mary when we had eaten pumpkin leaves as our only greens every day for a week. Yes, I had noticed! We didn't dare say anything to Massey though, for the only other vegetable available for many weeks was a fern that grew by the river. It not only tasted awful, but no matter how you cooked it, it was slimy! We preferred unpleasant furriness to slimyness any day.

Maw Dta would now teach us to appreciate many things. The first night in our tiny, cramped bamboo home we had only

Massey could always find something for us to eat—even if it was just leaves and bark and roots.

begun to unpack when the light began to fade. Where were the kerosene lamps? The kerosene itself was easy to find, for we had a five gallon can. But only when there was no more light in the sky was a lamp finally discovered. And of course, we had to wait for daylight to discover our matches!

Bathing in the river at Maw Dta was no real treat for us either. We were usually so careful about not losing our sarongs in the swift current that we didn't get very clean. Nor could I begin to count the bars of soap that slipped from our grasp, and before we could grab them, sailed away downstream.

To these awkward circumstances we could and did adjust. It was not the primitive living conditions that caused us to lose heart; it was something quite different that finally became an unbearable burden. Mary and I had gone to Maw Dta with pity — in answer to Maw Dta's request that had captured our hearts. So it shattered our enthusiasm to repeatedly observe the lives of Mrs. Maw Dta and her two daughters. Having been to a Christian school, they could quickly find most any passage of Scripture, read and expound on it. They could name off the disciples and even the kings of Israel in order. But then they would go home to mutter spirit incantations over the bones of an offering. They would invite us to have a meeting in one of their homes, and while we talked on the open porch an illegal still would be belching out the stench of liquor brewing in the inner room where we were never invited to go. This family could bless the village with their prayers, but when the prayers were ended they would slyly pass a bundle of raw opium to a waiting client. With their lips they blessed, but with their hands they cursed to a dreadful fate. They led us to heaven with their prayers, but with their lives they led the way to hell.

Mercifully, we were slow to understand what was happening. The language barrier fenced us in to an illusion, and we had ministered in love and pity to this family and their many neighbors. But with understanding, the illusion shattered and so did our pity and human love. To minister became a tedious burden. After two years there was no illusion, there was no joy of expectation in our hearts, and we felt we could turn our backs on the village of Maw Dta forever.

Only the old man whose name the village bore could we count as a Christian brother. When we first moved into his village his concept of God was a blasphemous confusion and he regarded the Bible as a magic charm. But even from the beginning he had a heart ready to hear, to receive, and to obey. We could not doubt that God had brought us to Maw Dta because He wanted us to teach and encourage *this one man.*

Maw Dta would always remind me of the picture of a tree stump found in the fourteenth chapter of the book of Job: "For there is hope for a tree, if it be cut down, that it will sprout again, and that it's tender branch will not cease. Though its root grow old in the earth, and its stock die in the ground, yet at the scent of water it will bud and bring forth boughs as a plant." Maw Dta was truly cut down. He surely appeared as a dry stump with no sign of life when we first met him. There seemed no hope and no life for this one so crippled in his Christian experience. But at the scent of water, the water of the Word of God, he began to bud and bring forth boughs as a plant. There was every evidence of real spiritual life and growth as he responded to the Word of God.

But there was no ministry that reached beyond this one man. Beyond us were the hills and mountains where hundreds of thousands of Karen lived in utter darkness, having never once heard the message of light. Most of them had never so much as heard the name of Jesus. That the God of creation loved them and gave His only begotten Son to die in their place, to lift them up to *His* place of endless life, was truth hidden to the blindness of spirit worship.

We had visited again and again not just the Karen of our own village but of every village we could reach within walking distance. Since without an invitation it was never acceptable for women to expect overnight hospitality from a Karen village, we had to be content to visit only those villages close enough for us to be able to get home before dark. And throughout that area we soon realized that we were considered teachers of the Maw Dta clan — and faces and hearts were closed and unresponsive. I reasoned in my heart that Maw Dta was not the village God would use to reach the hills beyond and I was reconciled to closing the door behind us.

Perhaps no village on the Burma side of the hills was usable as a starting point to reach the hill people either, I reasoned. The Karen in Burma had been engaged in warfare for over ten years. And to the Karen of those Thai hills this was a religious war — making that religion distasteful.

The Karen legends tell of their migration from the mountains of Tibet down across China to the mountains of Thailand and Burma. There were hundreds of years of constant moving until this nomadic people found the hills in Thailand and Burma to be the resting place their hearts could call home. Hundreds of families and separate villages had moved through alien lands, passing by other ethnic and language groups. Always the Karen remained detached, uninterested in the cultural groups they passed among during the long move to the south. Now at home in Thailand, the Karen did not interest themselves in the affairs of the Thai or any other tribal group. But their kinfolk across the border were so embroiled, so entangled with the nationals of Burma, that they were obliged to fight an endless war.

Watching the guerilla movement across the border, the Karen of Thailand judged that the Karen of Burma had accepted an alien religion, and that it was this Christian religion that forced them out of detachment into this involvement. They now had to fight a war that could never be won in order to practice that religion. These long years of fighting erected a barrier that closed out any attraction that the gospel might have had in Thailand.

I seriously doubted if the Thailand Karen living close to that war could hear the gospel at all. How could the voice of the Healer, the Helper, the Savior, the Comforter be heard above the hate and the anger and the acts of murder and mutilation being committed by "His people"?

I had also begun to feel that I was not usable in the Lord's hands to reach the Karen. I wondered if my own strong doctrinal background did not make it impossible for me to ever make the gospel anything but a foreign mystery to the Karen.

We had been given some gospel records to play to help us in the presentation of the gospel to the Karen. Most of them were a great help. But the one that was reported to be the most effective in reaching the spirit-worshiping Karen was the one that with every hearing I felt more strongly I could not use. It was the story which has been called the Legend of the Lost Book. This is a legend which has been passed down for centuries by Karen seated around the smoky open fireplaces of their mountain bamboo homes. I have heard many versions of it, but the basic story is always the same.

In the dawn of the world, father-god went away and left his sons. (Sometimes there are three sons, sometimes as many as seven, but always the white son is the youngest son.) The father leaves each of his sons a gold and silver book containing the answers to all of life's problems. The younger white son takes his book and leaves home. The Karen son is taken up with the cares of life and he does not read his book. He soon forgets all about it and does not even remember where he last laid it down. It falls beneath the house and the pigs root around it and the chickens scratch dirt over it, and the book is at last buried from sight. The legend always is the same at this next point: Someday the younger, white brother will come back and bring his book with him!

I had heard that this legend was used of God to prepare the hearts of the spirit-worshiping Karen in Burma for the coming of the white missionaries with the gospel. And because of this legend the gospel had not been foreign, but their own long-expected book. At first hearing, the story sounded good, but as I listened to the record and the talk of the Maw Dta Karen comparing different versions of the legend, I began to have disturbing doubts.

Suppose I held up the Bible and said, "This is that book!" Then I would seem to be giving assent to all of the story, and I could not do that. God the Creator does not stand in relation to His creation as a human father to his offspring. God has not deserted His creation; *we* are the ones who have gone astray. In some accounts of the legend the father puts a conditional curse on his sons if they do not keep the book. In Karen minds, the father's desertion and pronouncing of the curse puts him in the place of committing the first wrong. And later I was to realize that it was much more complicated than this. For in Karen thinking the two great spirits who inhabit eternity are male and female. Satan is female — and to this day harlots are often called by the name of Satan, for she is believed to exist eternally as a temptation to God! A heathen spirit doctor once told me what Karen take for granted: Satan was the mother of the sons of god in their legend of the lost book.

I could not preach the gospel from a heathen legend. I could not present the holiness, the love, the judgment or the forgiveness of God using a heathen Karen legend as an introduction to the gospel. I could not bend on this. If it was necessary to present the gospel in Karen terms against the background of legends before these people could hear, then I was just not at all suited to work among the Karen. God had led me to the wrong Bible school and to the wrong sources of fellowship if I was now to doctor up the gospel to appeal to a people whose appetites were whetted by dark legends.

If I were to come back after furlough and work again among the Karen, I surely did not want to come back to this same village or even this border area. Actually, I did not want to work with Karen at all. Perhaps my reasoning was an attempt to justify my longing to return to Maesod and a ministry among country Thai. Maesod had been such a fruitful and happy place of ministry for Mary and me. I longed just to forget the frustration of Maw Dta and return to Maesod.

Less than a month before Mary and I were to leave for furlough, a fire broke out in our village. There was an hour of terror that seemed to stretch on and on. House after house burst into flames in our tiny village. The scorching winds of the hot season had whipped into flame a smoldering fire where villagers had been smoking ants out of their nest and away from the delicious, succulent eggs. That harmless smoking log suddenly flared and became the torch, carried along by the wind, to set ablaze a string of houses.

Our village was twenty miles and at least twenty years away from a running-water system. Buckets and bamboo joints could not carry water fast enough from our dried-up river to do more than cool the ashes where fire had completely devoured a house, and barefoot villagers could only sift through whatever was left of their possessions, seeking anything that had not burned.

Mary and I were terrified as we stumbled down to the river with just our passports and official papers. Terror blinded and paralyzed us. I couldn't think of another thing in that house, soon to be destroyed, that I wanted to save. We just huddled with the other women and children of the village by the tiny flow of water.

We had already decided that when we left the village at the end of the month for the trip back to our respective countries for furlough, we would not choose to come back to *this* place. And the fire, blazing out of control, would soon destroy forever any sign that Christian missionaries had ever lived in this village. We had come two years earlier with every hope that here at the foot of the mountains overlooking Burma, God would use us to build a monument that would last for all eternity. Now all that we had built was just about to be wiped out forever. In my heart I had closed the door to Maw Dta behind me, and I could hang a sign on that door stamped "failure." Those years of failure had eaten away at my expectations just like the fire was eating away at house after house.

As I watched the fire blazing out of control, sending another row of houses into a towering blaze, it seemed to me to be *God* closing the doors that I had already tried to close. In just moments our house would be burned, and there would be nothing left to indicate that we had ever lived there.

A tiny house not twelve feet from ours was already ablaze and sending flames high above our roof. In just moments our house would explode into flames. Then suddenly the wind shifted. The rushing fire changed its course and veered around our house, passing it by. It raced up the hill, leaving behind a train of burning houses. I was numbed by the thing I had seen.

When the evening winds had died down and the fires were put out, nine houses had been destroyed in a horseshoe-shaped path around our house, and in the center we alone were left unburned. Only our roof had been destroyed — for the men of the village had battled just one step ahead of the fire, tearing off the dry-leaf roofs. Those roofs had been like piles of kindling, and just one wind-blown spark would cause them to suddenly ignite into a ball of flame. So except for its roof, there it stood: the only house of the village that was truly unwanted by its occupants. Yet God had spared it from the flames.

I will always remember the peace and calm when the frenzied activity of the terror was past. I will always be able to picture the burning-red sparks that flashed across the blackness of the night sky from the last lingering flames, eating away at the dead limb of a huge old tree high over us on the hillside. And in the stillness and peace of that hour the Lord dealt with my heart, leading me to think His thoughts and to change the course of my life.

With our roof gone, I had lain in bed that night with the starry heavens above me, and I had listened in my heart to the thoughts of God. Maw Dta was rejecting Him, but that did not mean He would stop inviting the villagers to Himself. The hills were deaf to His call, but that did not mean He would stop calling.

When the little band of missionaries on a survey trip happened on the village of Maw Dta years before, it appeared to be a village of the deaf — because the Karen could not understand the Thai of the missionaries. Now I knew that spiritually it was truly a village of the deaf. It did not matter how many times we had preached the gospel, the village had not yet heard. Clinging to their old superstitions, fear continually filled their minds. And offended with us, they had not yet tried to listen to what we had been trying so hard to communicate.

But it was their lostness, deafness, blindness and rejection of Him that committed the Lord to continue to seek and call them. If I was to let Him use me in His seeking these people, I must *return* to Maw Dta.

Chapter 5

Goaded to Move

I returned to Thailand and Maw Dta a year later, hugging in desperation the certainty that I had felt after the fire. I had then been so sure God would work in Maw Dta. While still a young Christian, I had been taught to move in the dark on what God has shown in the light. Well, now I felt the present and future of Maw Dta was utterly dark. But there had been that flash of light, that sure guidance and revealed path, and I would walk now in what I had seen.

During furlough, word came that headman Maw Dta had died. This man was the door of access to the closed Karen tribe. His death was surely a bigger and more meaningful circumstance than the shift in wind that spared our house from burning. It was Maw Dta who had invited us to live in his village. Without him, we didn't really have an invitation at all. His invitation was also our guarantee of protection. Two years in a Karen village was long enough for us to realize that we had to have the good will and protection of our neighbors. Maw Dta as headman could guarantee this. But without him, did we really have the right to claim protection?

So many memories of those two years before furlough gave every indication that we were not wanted. We did not deceive ourselves that the first six months would be easy, for those were the months of the monsoon. The wind would blow in from the Indian Ocean, sweep across Burma and into the western border area of Thailand, bringing torrents of rain. For six months we would have rain almost every day and some days it would rain all day. We had left Thailand for our furloughs just before the rains started, so hopefully Mary and I could now get back into the village before the rains washed out all the roads, cart tracks and paths.

During those months of monsoon we would do as we had done before. We would send a man to Maesod with our mail every two or three weeks. First class mail awaiting us there would then be picked up at the mission house. The man would have to carry our mail in a plastic bag over his head as he crossed the swollen rivers. For twenty miles he would climb hills and cross muddy rice fields and churning rivers, and then repeat the task. It was always at least a two-day trip, but if fever or flooding hampered the carrier it could be as long as a week before we saw him return with our mail. Many times we came to feel that friends and loved ones were not just separated from us by time and space — they were unreal, a part of life that had never really existed.

Mary and I corresponded during our furlough and planned to return to Maw Dta even though the man Maw Dta was no longer there. But we could not imagine that the village would hold any more promise of friendship or acceptance of us and our message than it had before. We no longer had any illusions about the romantic nobility of the villagers, nor had we any about our own saintly reactions to them.

But upon returning from furlough there came another change in the situation. Suddenly, that unburned house seemed to me to have no significance at all. Mary was not well. Considering her health, the British home base leaders of our mission advised that Mary not return to life in a primitive village. For the time being Mary would be joining another missionary in Thai work. This was a circumstance so shattering I could hardly take it in.

I knew that our mission policy had never been to send one woman alone into an area where there were no Christians. As a policy, I was in complete agreement. It never occurred to me that, moving as I was in response to the direction of the Lord,

He would lead me in a detour of mission policy!

I knew that had we missionaries met in conference just as I was to move into Maw Dta on my own, there would be those of the fellowship who would feel that it was a dangerous and foolish move. Others would have felt that if God were truly leading me back to Maw Dta, then He would, in His own time, supply a co-worker to go with me. Waiting on God is an important part of missions that we all recognize. Surely we need this discipline, otherwise we might think *we* could set the pace, that this was *our* work and *we* could make the program and manipulate people and circumstances to reach our aims and goals within our time schedule.

I valued the principles of fellowship of my mission and realized my need of that fellowship. But this was not the time of field conference. Our field leader was authorized to make the day-to-day decisions that could not wait for conference, and I had no doubt in my mind that I would soon receive a letter from him requesting that I postpone my return to Maw Dta until I had a co-worker. That was just fine with me. I knew that in time God would show His love for the village of Maw Dta. But I took it for granted that this was not the time God would reach out to the village through me.

I would have welcomed a letter from the field leader redirecting me. I would have taken it as from the Lord. But the letter did not come. I journeyed up-country from Bangkok, stopping at our mission stations that dotted the quickest route to the Karen, and I kept expecting that letter. Only in Maesod, the last station before Maw Dta, did the uncomfortable thought occur. "What if I'm not told to wait? Do I dare go in alone?" Such a possibility did not seem real.

I found in Maesod that Massey was eagerly awaiting my return. Every other day, when there was incoming traffic, she had watched the huge trucks that rolled in across the mountains from central Thailand and thought of me. Though she was dismayed that Mary would not be going with us, Massey felt that we should not delay but hasten to get into Maw Dta before the rains came. And I began to sense that God was hurrying us. I could see the huge storm clouds gathering above the mountains. If we were to get to Maw Dta before the rains came, I knew we must buy and pack sufficient supplies to last the rainy season. And we must hurriedly contact and hire oxcart owners to take us there. As fearful as the prospect of returning to Maw Dta without Mary and without the man Maw Dta was, I began to know beyond doubt that God was moving us and moving us quickly.

So we began the task of shopping for flour, lard, salt, sugar, dried milk, tea, coffee, peppers, onions, kerosene, matches, soap, all the medicines that might be needed, and toilet articles to last six months. Everything had to be wrapped in plastic in case the rain started while we were on the way.

Massey made the arrangements for the oxcarts and suddenly the time had come to go. No word had come from the field leader.

The night before we were to set out I slept at Massey's house, because we wanted to get started before daylight. That night I faced not the possibility but the fact: I was going again to live among a people who worshiped evil spirits. They were mostly a people who were just indifferent to my presence and message, but there were also those who were hostile.

I was frightened, but I was also absolutely convinced that God was in control and nothing had gotten out of hand for Him.

It was still dark and only the cocks were awake when our seven oxcarts started out the next morning. We had not gone far before the rubber "flip flops" I wore for shoes wore blisters on my feet and I was reduced to riding in one of those carts. Can there be anything to compare with the swaying, bouncing, lurching, jolting, jarring motion of an oxcart as it pitches its way across the ruts and ridges of a dry rice field? All day long I was trying to brace myself for the next sudden jolt or was squirming around to find the most comfortable position in the cramped cart.

When we started out there had seemed to be a thick, soft cushion of straw under me, and there had been a comfortably wide space between the cardboard cartons on one side and the kerosene cans on the other. The driver took up an amazingly small space at the front of the cart, and the woven bamboo roof he had erected as protection against the expected rains was sufficiently high so that I could sit without stooping. It was a strange thing, then, that not an hour later the straw had all worked its way out from under me. The cartons and fuel cans had begun to crowd in until I couldn't move at all without being pierced by a sharp corner or pinched by steel banding. The driver relaxed more and more, leaving me less and less room — and to add to my discomfort, that nice, high covering must have been slowly settling down, for stoop as I would, I still had my hair constantly tangling itself in the loose bamboo weave.

But it is reassuring to know that the oxcart that is hurtling one along is firmly constructed, and I tested the firmness of the construction for thirteen hours by bouncing up and down on it.

How often Mary and I had made this trip. We had walked it in the dry seasons. Starting out early in the morning, we found that walk to be cool at first, and fun at first. But in the heat of the day our enjoyment would evaporate as the trip stretched on and on. The journey was always too long, and we usually managed some accident along the way. One of us would either slip off the narrow, steep ridge partitioning a rice field or stumble on the sharp stones of the river or fall from some narrow bamboo footbridge spanning a gully. We would arrive at journey's end with scrapes and sores and the deeper aches of muscle and bone. But there were two of us, and when we stopped to rest we could talk of other places and times. I knew that I would miss Mary in many ways, but mostly I would miss her for her companionship.

After hours of walking through steaming jungles, Mary and I loved to sit on the ground under the shade of a tree and together join in refreshing laughter as she recounted episodes that had captured her humor as a girl, such as her story of the bike. Dressed in a hideous uniform and topped with a huge, flat-brimmed hat, Mary was returning to her boarding school. Mistaking a high British naval officer for a railroad official, she asked him to help her load her bicycle onto the train. Through her eyes I could see that impeccably groomed, proud member of one of the most elevated societies on earth. I could see his startled shock and affronted dignity at being so approached by a grubby schoolgirl, as Mary described herself. (Mary had explained to me, also, that the truly cultured British accent is as if a large plum were caught in the throat. The larger the plum, the more cultured the speech.) The poor naval officer, between his culture and his shock, could hardly speak at all. It was in a strangled gobble that he admonished her to find a railroad attendant and not a member of the king's navy.

I realized that had Mary stood on the dignity of her background, the life we had been living in Maw Dta was far more of an offense than the insult she had innocently offered to the naval officer. I missed Mary bitterly.

I knew I would also miss Mary as a nurse. But Mary was always like a nurse off-duty. The knowledge was there, the ability was there, but she never assumed that anyone wanted her advice or treatment until they asked for it. That had surely saved us many heartaches in Maw Dta.

We had taken in a certain amount of medical supplies when we first moved to Maw Dta, thinking that medical help was one of the ways we could serve the village. But the one who gave power to the spirit doctors was in tight control, and he did not release his grip. There were a few people who asked us for fever medicine, but even these usually repented of their bravery and never finished the dose or course of treatment. Visiting those she was treating, Mary would frequently find a certain forked branch at the foot of the bamboo ladder leading up to the patient's house. This was the sign that their home was closed to outsiders while they had the spirit doctor in, with his ceremonies and incantations.

I never saw Mary get irritated that people didn't take the medicine the way she told them to, or be upset that they turned from her treatment back to the spirit doctors. She seemed to be able to view the circumstances from their position. Why should they respect her nursing or opinion? Her approach to illness was utterly foreign.

However, children's sores and scratches, runny ears and red eyes were all brought to Mary. She gave them all the attention and care that the spirit doctors considered to be a waste of time.

Remembering Mary as a nurse now caused me as much inner discomfort as the bouncing oxcart caused my posterior. I am not a nurse and the thought of the village children, who always seemed to live at the very edge of the grave, was an overwhelming burden. Mary and I had watched and counted. More than half of the children born in the village had died within two weeks of birth. And more than half of those who survived the first two weeks died before reaching school age. (Though Maw Dta had no school, I still thought in terms of "school age.")

In case I should ever be allowed to help, I had brought a good supply of medicines. I knew it was most unlikely, however, that I could tell the difference between malaria, dengue or virus fevers. I could put ointment on sores and cuts and itches, but I would be pretty useless when it came to the illnesses that killed our children.

Along with treating the children's scrapes and sores, Mary had one other very busy nursing service. She gave a course of medicine to help opium addicts endure withdrawal symptoms. Only those who truly wished to be delivered from their addiction were willing to try Mary's cure, however. One of her patients had been a very elderly man whose name meant "grandfather sickly." Grandfather Sickly was considered to be a holy man, for he had built a very beautiful little pagoda on top of a steep hill. His followers toiled, cutting a stairway up the hillside, and with bricks and cement and white paint had created something beautiful to see but hideous to climb. Every year Thai and Karen came from miles around to climb up to the shrine with their offerings and prayers for rain and harvest and health.

Though this elderly gentleman was considered to be holy he was a desperate opium addict, and with failing health in his old age he began to fear his addiction was sapping his strength. So he came seeking Mary's medicine.

I guess it was his position as a holy man that caused him to value incantations on a par with medicine. In any case, he asked Mary to make a chant to her God for him. Mary, feeling that this was a marvelous opportunity to give him the gospel from Genesis to Revelation, started her prayer with the fall of Adam and Eve. She worked her way through the promise of a Savior, to His birth and life, and had come to the crucifixion. Her plan was to move on to the resurrection and in the full context of God's dealing with sinful man, commit Grandfather Sickly to Him for his health. Grandfather had become restless and felt surely Mary had forgotten the point of this chant she was making. He suddenly thumped her on the knee and admonished her, "Don't forget me!"

I don't know how Mary managed to continue her prayer, but she did, and Grandfather Sickly seemed quite pleased with it.

When he left us, Mary collapsed in laughter. For years after, if we were together when someone lost himself in a long, involved prayer, Mary would catch my eye afterwards and I knew she was hearing again Grandfather Sickly's "Don't forget me!"

What if any of the villagers did turn to me for medical help, for children's illness or the complications of opium cure? Nothing but a miracle of God would ever make me adequate in such a circumstance. Then I realized that nothing but a miracle of God's working in my heart could ever have made me willing for the trip I was then making. And nothing short of a continuous miracle of His working could keep me in Maw Dta.

As the day wore on, one of the oxen pulling one of the carts just gave up in weakness and sat down in the middle of the cart track. The drivers discussed at great length what should be done. The ox was just too old and weak, they decided. The cart load was divided among the other carts and I was given to understand that the weary old ox would be slaughtered and his flesh sold in the nearest town. No wonder some of the meat we had been able to buy from traders who passed through our area had been so tough!

I knew that the collapse of the ox would be considered an evil omen by the Karen of our village. How often they had abandoned a cleared field because of some such omen. How often they would return from a trip just barely begun because they saw a dead animal in the way, or even a live animal cutting across the path in front of them, seeming to warn them that their trip should be cut off. Well, I surely hoped that none of our Thai cart drivers would tell the Maw Dta villagers about that ox, for they would surely send us out of the village on the strength of the bad luck that omen promised.

As the day wore on, it became more and more unlikely that the drivers would talk to the villagers at all. The storm clouds were growing blacker and blacker as the mountains grew nearer. The heavy, sultry air began to be stirred by fresh winds from those mountains, and the cart drivers started to make plans to unload Massey and me at the village and return immediately. There was a river just an hour's journey from Maw Dta, and the drivers figured that if they did not get back across it that evening it might be months before it would be recrossable. Surely it was already raining in those hills ahead, and the river would be rising with the runoff from those mountain rains. Should they be caught behind that river for any length of time they would find that there was no longer a cart track to Maesod, as much of that track crossed rice fields that shortly would be flooded for planting.

My stomach began to churn at the thought of our drivers leaving Massey and me with all our stuff just dumped beneath the house. However, if they left us immediately, the villagers would have no way of getting rid of us for months, no matter how much they might object to our presence. It was not a comfortable prospect at all, yet it was all too likely that this was just what was going to happen to us.

At last, in the late afternoon, the mountains seemed to march up on either side of us, and as the light was beginning to fade from the sky, we could see that they had closed in behind us. The skyline that was visible was very familiar. It was "our mountain" now leaning over us just ahead, and at last it was our own village cart track leading down into the cluster of houses hidden beneath the great trees.

Suddenly the twilight was filled with voices and the pounding of bare feet running before the carts. "Our tall auntie has come back!" ("Auntie Tall" had become my Karen nickname.) There were welcoming hands to help us down from the carts, but the last light of the dying day showed that there were no adults in that welcoming crowd.

As they had planned, the cart drivers quickly unloaded us. Struggling up into the house with just what we would need that night, we could hear the rumble of the carts dying away in the distance. The sharp winds were suddenly heavy with rain, and Massey and I knew that we had made it into Maw Dta just in time.

All day I had watched my cart driver goad his oxen on, ever on. In the morning they were fresh and would have easily turned aside from the rutted track to feed on the lush green grass by the wayside. The goad with its sharp prick kept them on the straight. Later in the day they were just tired and wanted to stop and chew and rest, but the goad drove them on. I felt that I too had been driven when I longed to turn aside and stop. But if it was His love for the Karen that chose the path, it was His love for me that used that goad. If it was His love for the Karen that planned to bring them into His salvation, it was His love for me that chose me to be His messenger to them.

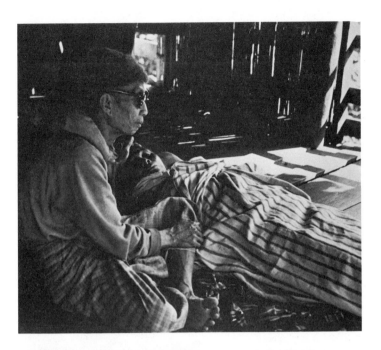

(1) *Maw Dta caring for his wife at a time of illness.*
(2) *Children gather on our porch.*

Chapter 6

A Grave in the Village

At four A.M. the rhythmic booming began. Where was I? Awakening out of a sound sleep, I was completely disoriented, for no trickle of light shone through the window to give a hint to the shape or sort of room I was sleeping in. But I had only to roll over and the soreness of cramped muscles reminded me of the past day's oxcart trip, and memory flooded back. I was on a makeshift bed, for there had been neither light nor energy to unpack bedding the night before. I was again in Maw Dta, and the booming sounds that filled the darkness were the young girls pounding rice for the day's meals. In just a few hours it would be far too hot for such strenuous labor. But at the last watch of the night, when often even the moon had passed from our heavens, the air was cool and moist . . . and that morning it was full of the smell of damp earth.

With awakening memories came excitement, for I remembered something Massey had been talking about the day before.

There was a grave in the center of Maw Dta's village. This was shocking. For generations, as far back as memory or tradition could reach, no Karen village had ever allowed a burial of the dead within a community of the living. But at Maw Dta's death all the heathen burial customs had been set aside completely, and a wooden cross marked his grave under flowering trees in the middle of the village.

In our area of the Karen world the dead are held in great

fear. All troubles and sorrows are believed to be caused by the spirits of the dead who return to their homes and communities to torment the living. There are chants and ceremonies and customs that must follow each death, with the hope of deceiving the spirit of the departed. The aim of every funeral is to get the spirit confused, out of the village, and lost in the forest so it cannot find its way home. At the end of three nights of spirit rites, four drunk men take the body away. Circling, retracing their steps and zig-zagging away from the familiar paths, they finally bury the body where it will never be found. The unmarked grave will soon be covered over by dense growth in the rainy season or by fallen leaves in the dry season. Even the men who bury the body can't be sure just where the grave is. In fact, they often are so drunk they don't know where the village is and have to spend the night lost in the forest. Of course, no one wants to find a grave, for a visitor to the grave would be followed back to the village by the spirit of the dead one. Then all those funeral customs practiced to disorient the dead would have been in vain.

Massey told me that all the chants and ceremonies had been canceled at Maw Dta's death, and the decision had been made to bury him in the village. I knew Maw Dta had been held in great respect, but respect cannot cancel out the sort of fear that binds Karen in darkness and torment at the death of a loved one. God alone could liberate these people to step outside the prison of their fear and make a mockery of their own sacred rites. Surely this grave in the village was canceling out all they professed to believe about death. I marveled that in death Maw Dta was still speaking to the family he so longed to win to the Lord in his lifetime.

I knew in that early morning hour that there were many in the village who had never heard the message that Mary and I brought them. Because we were so alien, our message could hardly be heard. Not only were we strange looking but strange sounding too, for they had never heard anyone that wasn't Karen speak their language before. They had never heard a foreign accent. When they finally understood the words so strangely pronounced, those words presented a foreign message. To people who live all their lives in the torment and fear of evil spirits, nothing could be more foreign than the message of God's holiness, His condemnation of sin, and His salvation for sinners. I felt sure that listening to us the villagers had not really heard us. But now they could surely hear the witness of the one they had buried in their village. How that thought encouraged my heart in the cool darkness of that morning!

With the brightness of day I learned of another surprising development. The night our oxcarts left Massey and me with all our belongings heaped beneath the house, the men of the village met in conference. The men who had buried Maw Dta were now plotting to bury my message.

I have liked to remind myself that God was as much in control of the decisions made by that group of heathen men as He is in control of our WEC conferences. It keeps my perspective right when I start looking at people and circumstances. They purposed evil but God purposed good, and He used their decisions to work out His purpose and not theirs.

They met, a dozen or more men, around an open fireplace in a bamboo house. The flickering fire and a smoky kerosene lantern would be all the light there was in that dark room. They would be literally voices lost in shadow. They met to decide how to deal with me, for I had come back uninvited and unwanted. They had no intention of accepting Maw Dta's religion, so I was an embarrassment to them and an unwanted responsibility. Out of respect to Grandfather Maw Dta they felt they could not ask me to get out. At least they could not do that directly. But Karen are past masters at the indirect, and in their conference they decided to tell me indirectly that it was useless for me to stay.

The men of the village decided to ignore entirely Massey's presence with me. Her testimony had made many of the Maw Dta clan uncomfortable and they chose to despise her rather than let her example convince them of their need of salvation.

In meeting together, the men of the village acted as if Massey was not with me at all. Their decision was to give me four teenage girls to live with me, explaining that it was not proper for me to live alone.

I realized that this was a slap in the face for Massey, and I was truly torn in my motives as the delegation from the meeting informed me of their decision. I surely wanted to be loyal to Massey, and I pointed out that I was not really alone, as she was living with me. But I was glad when the men dismissed that as unworthy of consideration at all. For to have four girls living with me in my home seemed to me to be a gift from heaven. What better opportunity of influencing anyone for Christ could I ever have in this world?

Massey did not seem to be at all hurt by the insult to herself, but was quite upset by the subtle plans she seemed to see in the offer of these particular girls. She felt certain that they would completely break my spirit, and at the end of the rainy season I would be ready to leave Maw Dta defeated.

Since the Karen custom is for young teenagers to either work at home or live with and work for neighbors and relatives, earning a salary usually paid in rice, it could not escape my notice that these four girls were not in demand at home or in the village. So on a level of deviousness that even I could see, I was expected to hire the unemployable. But since the rate of pay for such labor was about fifty cents a month, plus their food while they were living with me, I couldn't complain.

Three of the girls were first cousins and were granddaughters of Maw Dta. One was nicknamed "The Daydreamer." Later her mother told me that this girl was so absent-minded that the family felt she was retarded. She didn't respond to requests or commands and could not be used at all. In a society where even small children must help with household and farm chores, such a child is a severe burden.

The second girl was quick and obviously intelligent, but had such a bossy, commanding nature that she continually stirred up arguments and anger. The worst thing that can be said about a girl or woman in Karen society is that she is bossy. The men of the village were quite sure that they were effectively putting an end to any peace I could have in my household by giving me that girl.

The third of the cousins was a fat dumpling of a pre-teenager who was felt by the village to be turning out wrong. They judged that she was growing up to be just like her father. For years, Mang Way Bpa had acted as a killer for hire. Thai Buddhists who truly honor their religion will not even kill animals purposely. The devout bear a burden of guilt for even the bugs and ants they step on unknowingly. In most market towns of Thailand the Chinese operate the slaughterhouses, but even the most ardent Buddhist can buy and eat meat that has been killed for them. With the same reasoning — that if you pay someone else to commit the act it is not your sin but theirs — the Thai in our area turned to the animist Karen tribesmen to commit murder for them. If a man could no longer endure the presence of his enemy, it was a simple thing to visit a Karen village. A bit of conversation would reveal who were the "Karen guns." In those early days of my living in Maw Dta, ten dollars would hire a man to commit murder. The father of this third child was continually contacted in this way. His children were sent to buy whiskey from the neighbors and then serve it to their father and the men who came to seal the business transaction with him. The children of the household were thus constantly exposed to the plans of murder.

Ma Sing Way, the second daughter of that household, was already known as a thief. The village felt that she not only looked like her father but surely the same completely amoral spirit dwelt within her.

The fourth girl was not a member of the Maw Dta family clan at all. But Massey felt that she could see why her family was willing to give her up and why the men of the village should want to include her in the offer of four; she was a kleptomaniac. From the time she could walk she had begun to steal. She slyly tucked under her dress the most useless, valueless, senseless things. Her family was constantly embarrassed as they had to return the things she brought home. Beatings by her parents and older brothers and sisters and taunting and teasing by the other children of the village did no good at all.

The village feeling was unrestrained glee at the brilliant idea of giving me this child to live and work in my home. "If the foreigner thinks she knows the answer to sin, let her deal with this one."

In my ignorance I saw four normal, naughty gigglers ranging in age from twelve to fifteen years. I deeply appreciated them as a gift from the Lord. Certainly I planned to teach these girls all I could about the Lord Jesus Christ. But it was not my intention to start a children's work in a village that worshiped evil spirits. I knew that children were very much subject to the wishes of their parents, and I thought they would never be given the liberty to follow what their parents would term a "foreign religion."

I was greatly surprised then when Wa Paw, whose parents thought she was retarded, and Da Paw, whom the village considered too bossy, should immediately request to be baptized. When I questioned them, I found that each had a real Bible-based faith in Christ as Savior. They were aware of the Lord's acceptance of them and love for them, but at the same time they were experiencing constant conviction in the areas of their lives that displeased Him. I could not doubt that they had experienced salvation from sin's penalty and were just beginning the struggle to experience salvation from sin's power in their lives.

I would not have chosen to start the church of the Karen with two troubled children, but then I am not the Lord of the harvest. This was His doing.

I will never forget visiting the homes of those two girls and trying to explain what had happened. At Wa Paw's house I started a halting explanation that their daughter had come to faith in Christ as her Savior and was requesting baptism. I went on to say that I could not help but be glad for her faith for I truly believed in the judgment and hell that she now was secured against. But I said I realized that her faith would cause awkwardness in their home, as their practice was spirit worship. I never got any further. Wa Paw's mother, Mu Lay Moe (called such for the first child, who had died many years before

I came to Maw Dta), exploded. While the mother fumed in anger, Mu Lay Bpa settled against the house post in amusement. My embarrassment and his wife's anger delighted him no end. In saying their practice was spirit worship I was speaking the truth. But I had forgotten that Mu Lay Moe had been to a Christian school and had been baptized as a girl. She wished to maintain the facade that she was a Christian. Mu Lay Bpa was thoroughly entertained to hear his wife defending her position as a "Christian." Suddenly, almost the entire village was there to listen.

"What do you mean by accusing me of spirit worship? Why, my parents were baptized. I myself am a graduate of a Christian school and was baptized. And most certainly any of my children who want to can be baptized. Only my husband is a tree climber [the name for spirit worshipers in our area]. If you understood half of what is said in your presence, you certainly would know that I'm as baptized as you are!" If her words didn't fry me, the expression on her face ought to have done so.

I knew that, if anything, Mu Lay Moe was as renowned as a spirit doctor as was her husband. But I had not come to accuse her, and I felt sick that I had so offended her. The force of her anger and the ugly picture she presented of baptism without the working of the grace of God[1] made me feel quite ill.

I began to realize that apart from Grandfather Maw Dta, the other three of that family who made any claim to faith usually did not speak of themselves as "Christians" or "believers" or mention salvation or conversion or being born again. They spoke mainly of the fact that they had been baptized. Because I had come from a Baptist background, I found this unspeakably tragic. That people should so emphasize the sacrament and ignore the Savior was surely a disaster!

And then I realized the amazing door that Mu Lay Moe had opened in her anger. Wa Paw and Da Paw had requested baptism — but because of the Word of God that they had been hearing from their grandfather, and from Mary, Massey and myself, it was not just a request for a rite that showed a change of religion. They had experienced a change of life, and they understood the picture of baptism that spoke of their identification with Christ in His death, burial and resurrection. Mu Lay Moe's blast of anger was publicly giving me the go-ahead to teach her family. Had she not lost her temper and had her husband not been so pleased to see her testimony as a "Christian" so attacked, I'm sure they would have been much more cautious in their response. And I should not have received so wide an opportunity.

What happened at Da Paw's house was as embarrassing as the episode at Wa Paw's, but in an entirely different way. Though Da Paw's mother was also a daughter of Maw Dta, she had never had any Christian exposure at all until Mary and I moved into her village. Her father had brought her along to a few meetings before he died, but because she was quite deaf I'm sure she had not a clue as to what we were doing. I felt as if I were blasting off as loudly as Mu Lay Moe had done when I tried to talk to this woman. But I wasn't loud enough. Da Paw Moe asked, "Huh? Eh?" until I was about to lose my voice entirely with the strain. Finally her husband took pity on me and explained that though she was a bit deaf, his wife couldn't hear at all if she didn't want to. Yes, I could teach his children all I wanted. Be baptized? Sure! He had the testimony of two sisters-in-law that baptism made no real difference in a person's life.

He laid down the rules very carefully. Da Paw Bpa spoke with all the authority of a village elder when he explained that his children could be taught about Christianity but they would still have to take part in all the family worship ceremonies. They would have to "feed the spirits." They would have to have spirit strings tied to them to secure their own spirits to their bodies, and they would never be excused from any spirit ceremony. With dirty white strings wrapped round and round their wrists and necks, the immediate visual testimony they would present was fear of evil spirits and fear of death.

Da Paw Bpa's words fell with the weight of law, and I could hear them again and again over the next months.

"Who cares what the children think they believe? They will

have no liberty to obey their own convictions for many years. They are bound to carry out the convictions of their parents. And just you watch. When they are finally free to choose for themselves, they will go on with the ceremonies of their ancestors. It will no longer be their parents but the ceremonies themselves that bind them."

Da Paw Bpa's words disturbed me deeply, but I did have permission to go on and teach. And so with the four girls that lived with us, Massey and I would go out each morning to visit in different homes and in villages close by. We would tell the gospel stories and the parables of Christ. We would explain picture charts and flash cards and tell and retell the story of the cross and of the resurrection, the same stories I had told before with Mary.

One day we visited in Cad Way's village, a village just twenty minutes across the fields from Maw Dta. The girls urged me to visit a home and see a boy many believed to be the reincarnation of Maw Dta. I was horrified to look at the tiny boy clothed in filthy rags. His unwashed arms and legs were covered with mosquito bites that his dirty fingers had scratched into runny sores. Buffalo manure had been smeared on the top of his head to bring down a fever. His parents were both dull and the child seemed so slow and unresponsive that I felt certain that he was retarded. Maw Dta was a mature man with judgment and wit and compassion. What consolation, what comfort could this pitiful baby bring to those who were grieving for the man? Even if the baby had been clean and healthy and bright, he was still a baby. He could not be any sort of companion or friend to those who had loved Maw Dta.

If Maw Dta had really returned as this heathen baby, and would return again and again, never to remember past lives or loved ones, what was the point of our Lord's death? Why should He give His body to be broken or His blood to be poured out? What difference does it make to have sins forgiven in one life if we must come back to start all over again without understanding or remembrance? Reincarnation seemed to me more cruel than the grave, for the eyes of that baby looked back at Maw Dta's loved ones not only without recognition but without interest. As I listened to the talk about reincarnation I realized it held no hope of resurrection, but rather an eternity of senseless return with not only no memory or recognition of loved ones, there was not even *self*-recognition. Reincarnation offers only an eternity of lost identity. How can there be a Savior in reincarnation when there is no identity to be saved?

I felt I had looked into the depths of the despair and darkness of spirit worship when I looked into the eyes of that baby, believed by many to be the reincarnation of Maw Dta. I could have given up right then. I could have doubted right then that those people could ever come to faith. But something had started in my own home. Before even a week had passed, the other two girls had come to faith and committed their lives to the Lord. Wa Paw ("retarded") soon led her younger sister to the Lord. Da Paw ("bossy") led her younger brother to the Lord. And suddenly I had a group of saved young people, all eager to learn and grow in the Lord.

At the close of my first two weeks back in Maw Dta, a neighbor man was willing to carry my mail to the missionaries' home in Maesod. When he returned, how glad I was to see letters from my family and friends in America, a letter from Mary settled on a Thai station, a letter from Ellen who had lived with me years ago in Maesod, and yes, there it was, the letter from the field leader telling me not to go into Maw Dta just yet. Surely God would give me a co-worker before I should take that step into isolation. The letter had been delayed, and that was no accident. God was in control. For before a mail carrier could go out to inform the field leader of the fact that I was already in the village, I could report that Maw Dta was no longer a place without any Christians for there were several young people who were believers. It would be many months before one of the men missionaries could visit and conduct a baptismal service for us; but after the emphasis put on baptism by the Maw Dta clan, I was glad we didn't have to face that event just yet.

Writing this years after the conversion of the four girls who lived with me, it would be so easy to present the salvation experience of those four as so glorious that the village was electrified by the dramatic change in their lives. But that would not be true. The real truth is that they were girls with problems, and they became Christians with problems. Yet there was a substantial change in each of them. A change that could be seen and *was* seen; a change that could be talked about and *was* talked about. And they were changes that could not be explained by anything in Karen experience. The village adults watched and talked. I have often wished that I could have heard the conversations that went on until late at night around the open fires in the bamboo houses of Maw Dta. I have thought that those conversations might have been an encouragement to me, when month after month there was no response from the adults in the village. But then, maybe if I had heard the talk it might have just added to my frustration, for so often since then I have heard just that sort of conversation where heathen Karen families *sound* as if they are going to talk themselves right into faith. Of course, it never happens that way, for "faith cometh by hearing and hearing by the Word of God." Faith never seems to come by talking. While the adults talked, the children and young people heard and came to faith.

I could not help but wonder, what were the leaders of the village really considering? Were they considering the testimony of changed lives, or the fact of a filthy, sickly baby thought to be Maw Dta? Were they listening to their own superstitions or to the testimony of a grave in their village?

Chapter 7

Under a Microscope

Census takers had come to the village the first year Mary and I lived there. Knowing they had come up against a barrier and no longer would find their own language spoken, but rather a collection of tribal tongues, they were unwilling to go further into the unknown hills. But they needed to estimate how many Karen there were, uncounted, beyond the reach of the Thai government. The men of the village were summoned to gather at a very official meeting on our front porch. Then the census takers spread out a map. Running his finger along the mountains marked on the map, the spokesman for the group asked the men of the village how many people were in that area. The Karen were aghast!

"Who could live on that little bit of paper?"

"It's that Thai whiskey," one man muttered darkly as he abandoned those foolish questioners.

It is no wonder that in those days there was not even an educated guess of how many Karen there were in that area of the mountains bordering Burma.

Though it did appear that we were a people uncounted and unclaimed, when I remembered the spirit worship that ruled the hills I realized that we were a people numbered, not one overlooked. We were a people governed by a dreadful ruler, for beyond the roads and trails of Thailand the most ancient slavery of all numbered and controlled every living person.

The basic thought in spirit worship is that the unseen world all around us is evil. And this evil unseen world governs all that can be seen.

The Karen do believe in a good God of creation, and though their definition of good falls far short of the Biblical concept, through all our hills it was believed that man, basically bad, could not please or reach this God. Because of our evilness we are His abandoned creation. While He wants nothing to do with us and will not hear our cries, we are surrounded by evil spirits who touch us and can be touched by us. Every painful experience, every frustrated plan, every sorrow is the direct attack of these unseen beings.

The worship of evil spirits is never a matter of love or thankfulness but is always motivated by fear. There is always a desperate race to appease offended spirits before they have worked out their full plans. We can never win their friendship or cooperation; we can only hope to turn them aside from the evil they devise for us. This is the rationale behind spirit worship for most of the Karen in Thailand.

For the spirit doctors there is another level of approach to the spirits. Standing between their neighbors who want to appease the spirits and the spirits who want to harm and kill, they seek by trickery and deceit to manipulate the spirits into doing their will. There were powerful spirit doctors in Maw Dta. This did not mean that these men and women were in any way released from the bondage of fear that held their neighbors. No, the powers they had contacted in the spirit world held them unmistakably captive. For them there was a heightened awareness of the spirit world and, if anything, they lived in a worse torment than their neighbors who had never known power in the demon world. And the burden of unfulfilled promises, false claims and lies they had made to the spirits caused them to walk always in fear of imminent retribution.

When I returned from my first furlough I was keenly aware that I was dreadfully ignorant of the occult and black magic practiced all around me. I wondered if I shouldn't study the rules and claims of this dark system in order to fight it. But the very thought made me so uncomfortable I could not feel that the Lord was leading or encouraging me in this course.

I had only a narrow view of spirit worship — a view I believe God gave me in order to protect me from either fear of the dark powers or disgust at those held in the bondage of those powers. I saw the revolting blood sacrifices as counterfeits of "the Lamb of God that taketh away the sin of the world." I saw every incantation as an ugly perversion of the access every Christian has to the Father through prayer. I saw every ceremony as a distorted counterfeit of the Old Testament observances that were finished at Calvary. All of spirit worship I saw as a counterfeit way leading away from God.

To understand spirit worship in this light delivered me from considering men or groups of men as my enemies. They were, rather, "the deceived." I was not there to fight against them but for them.

I did not set out purposely to force a confrontation with spirit worship, but without meaning to do so I did bring things to a crisis. From furlough I brought a large metal drum of used clothing for the children of the village. I was not trying to change Karen customs of dress, for there would be just one or two changes of clothing for each of the children. Without regular washings with soap, I knew, these things would not last for long. But I enjoyed seeing the children's pride and delight in their foreign finery.

I soon saw that the older girls, who were already weaving their own coarse cotton dresses, were beginning to speculate. The lightweight cotton clothing I had given them was not all that different from the material used in the blouses and skirts that the Thai sometimes came selling through our area. They had never considered that those clothes would be more comfortable in the hot weather and that they would dry so much more quickly in the rainy season. But they now did begin to figure costs, and soon came to the conclusion that to buy heavy thread for weaving plus the value of the hours spent before their looms meant the wrap-around skirts and soft blouses of the Thai were not much more expensive than their own tribal dress.

Girls who did not live with me and earn the princely sum of fifty cents a month began to ask for work. They volunteered to cut weeds, carry water, make charcoal and pound rice. Others brought vegetables and spices from their fields to sell. In just a few weeks it was apparent that the girls of the village had chosen to wear the Thai dress instead of their tribal costume. Since their parents did not seem to mind, I couldn't see why I should try to preserve a way of dress that was very ugly, impractical and uncomfortable.

And then we had a funeral in the village and the crisis was upon us. I found that at a heathen funeral where evil spirits must be appeased there must be several virgins dressed in new white dresses for a part of the funeral chanting. The virgins must be young, still in their teens or early twenties. An unmarried lady beyond that age is thought to be mentally deficient or physically handicapped and could not be acceptable to the spirits. (Now I knew what the village thought of me!)

The plainness of the virgin's dress — a straight sack with a little bit of fringe decoration — had its significance in spirit worship. Usually the thread is no longer white by the time the dress is woven (with dirty fingers), and I found also that the rule regarding newness was different than I expected. It did not matter how long a girl had been wearing her dress; in fact, she could have been wearing it to slop hogs in for six months and it was still "new." But if she had worn her dress even once into the rice fields to plant or harvest, it was no longer new.

Even though it was a compromised idea of white and a modified idea of new, not one young girl of Maw Dta now had a new white dress to wear for the funeral. Since the dresses worn at a funeral cannot be borrowed but must be woven by the girls themselves, no girl in Maw Dta could take part in the funeral.

Da Paw Bpa and Mu Lay Bpa did not hide their anger as they told me what a disgraceful situation had come about because of my influence. Now they would have to go to the villages further up in the hills to find girls willing to come for the funeral. They would lose face before the hills, and it was obvious that they were not about to forgive me in a hurry.

The girls who lived with me were truly sorry and planned right away to start weaving new white dresses. But after the first night of the funeral chanting not one word was spoken of the need for Karen dresses. Weeks later I asked Wa Paw if she was weaving a new dress at home. I was flabbergasted when she answered no, her father didn't want her to. She went on to explain, "He really listened to the virgins' chants at that funeral and now he doesn't want me or my sisters to ever take part again."

The funeral chants are learned by the tiny children of the village almost a dozen years before they would be eligible to take part in a funeral. They are chanted at play by little ones who cannot possible understand them. Though the rhymes are a bit obscure, it is really the familiarity that causes the Karen not to listen to the meaning of their own chants.

Evidently several of the men in the village really listened to those imported girls in a way that they would never have listened to their own daughters or sisters. For the first time in their lives they understood what they were requiring of their girls and they were appalled. And yet they might have guessed the truth, for what I learned of the funeral chant was much in keeping with the entire picture of spirit worship.

As the men listened in horror they realized that the girls were inviting the spirit of the dead one to possess them. Young and chaste and clean, they were calling upon the spirit, believed to be furiously angry with the living, to choose one of them to indwell. This is thought to forestall the spirit from possessing some strong young man the village leaders would not be able to restrain until he had done horrible damage to lives and property. I believe that with that first understanding of the virgins' funeral chant, some of the men of the village began to examine the meaning behind the rules and practices of their worship. But it would be many months before I would hear of their dissatisfaction with that dark way.

The men of the village were not only critically examining their own religious traditions, but the spotlight of constant observation and the magnifying glass of critical comparison was continually on the four girls who lived with me. Every conversation overheard and every action observed was magnified as the village discussed the changes in the lives of the four.

It was Wa Paw that was causing the most stir in the village, for Wa Paw was so completely changed. The picture was that of a girl in her early teens who seemed retarded and then suddenly woke up and showed herself to be bright, helpful and cheerful. In less than a month Wa Paw had learned to read and began to help me teach the younger children.

I'm sure that most of the village felt that the foreigner's God had healed the child's crippled mind. But I knew that the change was not the miracle the village thought it was. Wa Paw never was slow, but she was stubborn and rebellious and she existed in a shell of wounded dignity. Part of the problem was that Wa Paw was the fourth daughter of her house. Two of her older sisters had died before she was born. And there would be four more sisters before a boy would be born in that family. So for many years Wa Paw was called "Son" by her parents. As soon as she was able to do so, she let everyone know that she hated to be dressed as a boy, to have her hair cut as a boy, and above all, to be called "Son." Her parents had just ignored her when she told them she did not want to be called "Son," so she ignored them. As long as they went on treating her as a boy, she refused to do any of the things required of little girls.

Naturally I never even thought of calling Wa Paw "Son." Within Karen culture it was all right for me to call all the girls living with me "Niece" or "Daughter." Since daughter is a less cumbersome word than niece, I slipped into the habit of calling them all "Daughter." Wa Paw responded to "Daughter" with quick obedience. But there was also another reason for Wa Paw to respond just then and to prove that she was in no way retarded. Wa Paw was beginning to notice boys.

To Karen, marriage is first of all a business transaction. A girl's family is looking for a strong farmer or a young man with enough wealth to feed them all. The boy and his family are also looking for advantageous connections. But the primary thing a boy from a poor family would expect from his bride would be health and strength and all the housewifely skills. Tiny girls are taught to pound rice and how to cook it to perfection. Little girls can pound peppers until the paste is so smooth that not one pepper seed is seen. Older girls are taught to spin thread, arrange it on their looms, and weave their first plain white dresses. Later they learn to weave intricate designs (most of which are patterned after snake skins). Wa Paw should have known how to do all those things, but in her rebellion against being called "Son" she had refused even to observe the skills she should have been developing. Now, at last, the taunts that she would never be able to get a husband were getting through to Wa Paw, and she was smart enough to see that her stubbornness was hurting her.

Though I realized that the change that was so apparent was not a great miracle, I knew that there was behind that change a real work of grace that the village could not appreciate. It was not marvelous for Wa Paw to suddenly show that she was bright and could be industrious; what *was* marvelous was that this very proud little girl let go of her bitterness and let the Lord deliver her from an offended spirit.

Years later, when she was attending a school far to the north of us, while her father Mu Lay Bpa was visiting he slipped and called Wa Paw "Son." Naturally her friends at school began to tease her about this and Wa Paw was embarrassed almost to tears. But she had been delivered from bitterness about this early in her conversion, and she was able not only to laugh about it but so truly saw the joke that she told us all about it when she came home. It was not just a laugh of embarrassment but a laugh of entertainment, and she wanted to share it with us. At the same school one of the teachers told Wa Paw that her voice sounded like a cracked pot. The old Wa Paw would have been so offended that she would have quit school and come home in a huff, and no one ever would have known what hurt her feelings. But the Wa Paw in whom the grace of God was constantly working deliverance from an easily insulted and offended spirit could hardly wait for vacation to tell us all. She thought it was a great joke to be told that her singing voice sounded like a cracked pot! Truly it was a miracle for this proud, easily insulted child to learn to laugh at herself.

Naw Boo (the kleptomaniac) also was causing comment in the village. I do not at all understand what caused Naw Boo to steal things that she herself did not want. But I have seen over the years that when she is secure and happy she does not take things. If she is troubled and worried, she cannot seem to control herself. At the time of her conversion and for several years afterward, she was so undisturbed it looked as if she would never steal again. The lapses she has had have always been at times of great disturbance for her. The Lord has undertaken at such times of distress and has seen to it that Naw Boo has been surrounded by those who love her and shield her from ridicule.

Ma Sing Way (believed to be turning out bad like her father) became a believer along with her older sister, Mang Way. The father, who was in prison at the time of his daughters' conversion, came home only to return to opium and theft. He also began talking about killing those who were responsible for his arrest. Though he had been available to the Thai as a murderer for hire for years, he had never been known to kill a Karen. Now he was blaming the men of Maw Dta for his imprisonment, so it was not surprising that one rainy night a volley of shots rang out from the fields beside the village. We were told the next morning that Mang Way Bpa's body had been found riddled with bullets.

Though the widow and children were not told of his death for several days, they were the first to be affected by his absence. Almost all day and every night Mang Way Bpa had smoked opium in their tiny bamboo house. Often the house had been so full of his opium-smoking friends that there was hardly room for his wife and six children to stretch out to sleep. Immediately after Mang Way Bpa's death the entire family became ill with chills and fever, aches and pains, vomiting and diarrhea. Since the mother and all six children were violently ill, it looked like something contagious, yet no one else in the village seemed to be affected. Suddenly I realized that their illness seemed very much like the withdrawal symptoms of some of the men Mary had helped to break off from opium. A bit of visiting around the village and my suspicions were confirmed. I found that most certainly it is easy to become addicted to the opium smoke in a poorly ventilated room.

When Mary had given a cure to opium addicts, their women and children had often suffered more withdrawal symptoms than the smokers, I was told. I knew the dosage Mary had given men, but working out a dosage of a strong drug for small children was surely more of a responsibility than I wanted to take. Yet how could I stand by and see them suffer without helping? Neighbors reminded me that lovely little children long gone from the earth had died because their opium smoke was taken away when their fathers left the village for a logging season. I suppose the actual deaths were caused by malaria or pneumonia, but surely the opium withdrawal symptoms complicated and increased their suffering.

With caution and prayer I started the treatment by using such a small dosage with the children that their symptoms were barely lessened. Yet in the graciousness of the Lord the medicine was enough and the family quickly recovered.

Ma Sing Way was a very affectionate, responsive child. Her father, the selfish opium sot, had been first in her affections for years and it is no wonder that her actions had been a faithful copy of his morals and goals. With conversion this responsive child put Jesus Christ first, and the about-face of her outward conduct was staggering.

Da Paw (the bossy one) was the one whose observable life sent out the most confusing signals. And that was no wonder. At the beginning of her walk with the Lord her father told me Da Paw could be baptized. But long before one of the men from WEC would come to perform that service, Da Paw's father had changed his mind. He told her she could never take part in any Christian ceremony. He didn't care what she learned of Christian teaching, but she was to do nothing that would bind her to faith in or practice of this foreign religion.

Da Paw Bpa was very ill with what would later be revealed to be tuberculosis. In the early stages of his illness his discomfort showed itself in his erratic treatment of his teenage daughter. He would one moment praise his daughter and the next he would order her out of his home, telling her he counted her as dead and never wanted to see her face or hear her voice again. For days at a time the tormented child would not go near her house. This rejection in her home was so traumatic an experience for Da Paw and so deeply upset her that for months she was unable even to begin to learn to read the Karen alphabet. When the other young people were reading the Scriptures, Da Paw was still unable to read her own name. This surely added to her distress, for she was the oldest of the Christian young people.

Da Paw's bossiness was the spontaneous expression of her quick mind: seeing what needed to be done and how to do it. When happy, Da Paw's commands flowed unchecked and the saving grace was that she wasn't offended when her ideas were rejected. But the unhappy Da Paw was cowed. If Da Paw had been a puppy, everyone would have understood her. Drooping ears and tail would have signaled to all her rejection and misery. Bumptious barking and wagging tail would have told of her acceptance and happiness. But the girl — one day quiet, hardly aware of her surroundings, and the next day laughing and bossy — confused the watching village. They could not understand. It had nothing to do with her religion that Da Paw was so erratic. It was her earthly father and not her Heavenly Father that caused the changes in the girl's actions.

I knew we were all under the microscope of the watching eyes of the villagers and could not help but wonder what they saw and how they interpreted what they saw. Were they attracted or were they repulsed?

Chapter 8

The Despised and Rejected

The first few weeks back in Maw Dta after furlough I continued to hope that Mary would recover her physical stamina and return to work with me. As long as it was only a physical condition that kept Mary from Maw Dta, I could hope for her return. But as the months passed, God closed the door to Maw Dta behind Mary and began to open a door into a literature ministry in Bangkok. From a pre-evangelistic ministry to the unresponsive Karen people, she was moved to serve the hunger of the growing Christian community all over Thailand.

Mary could joke about "mud-hutting it" when she visited Maw Dta, but it was true. God had moved her from the hills, sleeping a thousand years behind the times, to Bangkok, in the contemporary race with every major metropolis in the world. God moved Mary from charcoal firepots and smoky kerosene lamps to electricity and air conditioning; from a river and buckets to hot and cold running water; from lonely, quiet footpaths to traffic jams with the pollution and noise of a thousand stalled cars; from an illiterate, unevangelized people to a literate church, hungry for the printed page.

Since God was leading I had to accept it. Mary would only come to Maw Dta as a well-loved guest and never again as a co-worker. But when there were two of us, we had been a pitifully weak force, and now even that force had been cut in half.

What a measly few we were that met week by week to worship the Lord. Our very singing of hymns, reading of Scripture and praying to the Most High God was in defiance of the powers of darkness that held all that mountain world in the fear of death. How ridiculous it seemed that such a puny, no-account band should so challenge the prince of the power of the air.

The little group of believers meeting for worship and to learn of the Lord was mostly young people, some with deep problems of personality. Some had pressing family problems and it was all they could do to continually claim cleansing for wrong actions and attitudes. They couldn't love a lost world when they couldn't even truly love a lost father or brother. Maybe they felt strong family love, but it was so hard to act out that love while they were being ridiculed and rejected.

There was a tiny group of adults who claimed salvation, but they seemed to have more problems than the young people. Though they had turned from the dark occult practices that had ruled them all of their lives, it seemed to me that they had not turned all the way to a loving, intimate relationship with the Lord.

Ja Bee Moe was a widow who often met with us. Her husband went insane and was chained to a bamboo thicket with elephant chains before his death. Massey had pointed out to Mary and me during that time of trauma and distress that this woman with two small children to feed and care for was also in desperate physical need. So we had supplied food and clothing for the little family and had made provision for them when we went on furlough.

We did not befriend her just to win her soul. Her need was reason enough. And there was no one else to help. But I am sure that Ja Bee Moe felt obligated to embrace Christianity because of that help. Mary and I felt that in the very way she expressed faith in God it was obvious that she did not know what it was all about. We were told that she fed the evil spirits when we were away from the village, and when her husband died Ja Bee Moe began to sleep with a sharp knife to protect herself from his insane spirit.

The Peterses wrote that Ja Bee Moe had come to faith while we were on furlough. Reading their letter, I thought back to the many times she had expressed faith in the Lord only to return to the fears of animism. I hardly knew what to expect, but returning from furlough I found Ja Bee Moe with spirit strings at her neck and wrists. Praying with the Peterses, this troubled woman had still come short of real saving faith that would deliver her from the bondage of spirit worship. She was still saying and doing what she hoped would please whoever she was with.

It was a burden to me that there was nothing in Ja Bee Moe's life to validate her claims of faith in Christ as Savior. But I could not understand why an unbelieving village should absolutely dismiss her and any testimony she would give. Then I learned something of Ja Bee Moe's past.

I realized that Ja Bee Moe had a very weak mentality and I thought perhaps this was caused by her husband's breakdown and death. But those who had known her for many years told me what had happened after the death of a previous husband. She had traded an elephant for a water buffalo! (A water buffalo is only worth a tenth of the price of an elephant.) Her irate family realized that she was no longer competent when they found this out. Ja Bee Moe was kept under close care after that, and all her affairs were managed for her until a second husband came along to take care of her. It is no wonder that she fell apart mentally when he went insane.

I saw a needy woman whose needs were barely touched on the physical and material levels and I sorrowed that she did not have a vital testimony of her needs being fully supplied in the Lord. But the village was watching a women who could trade an elephant for a buffalo. They expected the ridiculous from Ja Bee Moe and would never have accepted as genuine any testimony she could give.

Moses' Mother (her original name was Ee Kay Moe) was another widow who chose to worship with us. Until Mary and I left for furlough her husband had been alive, and he had forbidden his wife to become a Christian. She told us, however, that she believed our report and was trusting the Lord for salvation. When her husband died she would be baptized, she proclaimed. That seemed a rather extreme pronouncement, considering that her husband was quite young and, though an opium addict, seemed in good health.

The village people felt that this woman had a valid testimony in that when the fire raged through the village destroying house after house, her tiny bamboo home, right in the path of the fire, did not burn. The two houses on either side of her house were burned right down to the ground, but sandwiched in between, Moses' Mother's house was left without a scorch. She maintained that it was in answer to her prayer to the God of creation that her house was spared. And the village seemed to accept her testimony.

While we were away on furlough, Moses' Mother's husband became ill. Weakened by opium addiction, he suddenly died. Shortly after his father's death, Moses was born. In the Lord's planning, Bill and Rosemary Charters, our missionary replacements in Maesod, were visiting the village at the time of this very sickly little boy's birth. They gave help to the mother that surely saved the life of the baby. Moses was named by the Charterses, and they were thrilled that his mother followed through on her promise. Though she was not immediately baptized, she did cut off her spirit strings and learned to pray after encouragement from Bill and Rosemary. Because of the language barrier, however, Bill Charters did not feel he could assess her understanding or faith, and he did not want to carry out a premature baptism. The Charterses had taken a few months of Karen study in order to support the Peterses, Mary and me. But with limited vocabulary they were not only often unsure of what the Karen were saying to them, they were at times unsure of what they were saying themselves.

Though the villagers believed that God had answered Moses' Mother when she prayed during the fire, they were still skeptical about her claim to faith. They noted that this woman who talked of an all-powerful God yet had water blown over Moses by a spirit doctor just like any other baby of the village.

"Ja Bee Moe and Moses' Mother can walk in two directions at the same time," the village people laughed. "So can the young people who say they are Christians." The villagers felt sure that they were soon to see the foreigner go and the young people turn back from the foreigner's way. But I felt sure that though the two widow women still saw the gospel as an alternate way, the young people saw it as it was, God's *only* way.

Bay Law Moe and her husband were our first professing Christian couple, and how I hoped that they would be victorious Christians, claiming all that Christ had done for them. They should have been a balanced, normal couple who, starting with a healthy emotional life, could go on to a more outgoing, loving, giving, responsive Christian life. At least that is what I thought. But that is not what I saw. I did not even begin to know their story until after the first few months of their Christian life.

Bay Law Bpa was the brother and only living relative of the young man who had been put to death for sexually assaulting two children. He was almost neurotic, he was so torn between shame at what his brother had done and the desire to avenge his brother's blood.

Bay Law Moe, I thought, was Maw Dta's youngest daughter. But I was told finally that she was not really a daughter of Maw Dta at all. This was the child conceived when Maw Dta was away logging years before. Though now grown and married and the mother of Bay Law, there was no doubt that the woman was crippled emotionally because of the stigma and rejection brought on by that long-ago sin. As her husband bore in his personality the results of his brother's ugly sin, Bay Law Moe was embittered by the cruel ridicule of her own family and village for her mother's sin.

Somewhere along the line I had picked up the foolish notion that backward people do not have the same problems of more civilized people. How naive! Sin is the same and always works the same long process of death. The sin-death process was all about me in Maw Dta with its stages of tension, fear, jealousy, anger, resentment, bitterness and defeat. And it seemed to me that this little group that called themselves Christian had more problems and scars than anyone else. If it was their problems that caused them to be drawn to the gospel, it was also their problems that kept them back from a total commitment to the Lord.

The little group of believers in Maw Dta had been meeting for fully a year before Bill and Rosemary Charters visited us, and Bill now agreed to perform a baptismal service for us. There were several young people and three adults who understood what it meant to follow the Lord in public testimony of their union with Him in His death, burial and resurrection. Moses' Mother along with Bay Law Moe and Bay Law Bpa were the adults of that group. Though there were more than a dozen young people who were responding to the Lord with firm purpose to obey Him completely, there were only five of that group whose parents would permit them to take so public a stand as baptism. All five of these were grandchildren of Maw Dta. Although the little old headman was gone from the earth, it was his influence that opened the way for his grandchildren to obey the Lord. Christian young people who were not Maw Dta's descendants would now stand by unable to do anything more than believe in their hearts and speak out only the briefest expression of their faith. How thankful I was then for that verse in Romans chapter ten, "For with the heart man believeth unto righteousness, and with the mouth confession is made unto salvation." Even if they never had liberty to be baptized, belief had been born in their hearts and expressed by their mouths. Their salvation was sure.

Baptism was far more of a test for each of the candidates than I ever could have imagined. For Da Paw ("bossy") it was the start of months of silence during which her father would not even acknowledge her presence in the village. He had given his permission for Da Paw to be baptized in that he said to her, "Sure, go ahead, but I will count you as dead." And Da Paw's father never so much as spoke to his daughter again until the day he died almost a year after her baptism. Though she helped nurse him in the last weeks of tuberculosis, he would not look at her. If I had understood the heartache and the rift that was forged in that home, I'm sure I would have urged Da Paw to postpone her baptism. I'm glad I never knew, for I would have been wrong. Da Paw had the settled assurance that she gave her father respect and love but also never compromised her testimony. Da Paw Bpa not only heard the gospel but saw how completely his daughter was committed to the Lord of the gospel. Da Paw Moe came to tell me on the very day her husband was buried that she now had come to faith because of her daughter's faithfulness, which surely indicated that Da Paw was not acting in unreasonable disregard of her father's wishes. In fact, the verdict of the village over the years has been that having once come to faith, there never was any way Da Paw could have pleased her father. His displeasure was a complete barrier that she could never have overcome short of verbally denouncing the Lord. To postpone her baptism would have made no difference in the situation. Da Paw surely stood in the place of the rejected.

Wa Paw ("retarded") had her problems too. Her father, Mu Lay Bpa, teased her about "seeing God," telling her that that was what baptism was all about: when she went under the water she must open her eyes and she would see God. If she did not see Him, the baptism was no good and she would have to go under the water again. He told a fascinated audience on their porch of how as a young boy he had met Baptists from Burma. Afterwards he had "baptized" all the smaller boys in his village. One poor, wee soul he had dunked again and again. Each time he raised the little boy he asked, "Did you see God?" The poor sputtering, crying, half-drowned little boy finally answered "Yes," so he was at last set free.

Wa Paw's father turned it all into a joke. But it was Mu Lay Moe who knew how to really hurt. Having been to a Christian school, there was nothing her daughter could tell her of the way of the Lord that she had not learned in theory as a girl. Her response to Wa Paw was always that such a religion was exciting and challenging for a young girl, but had no part in real day-to-day living. She dismissed Wa Paw's testimony, implying that the girl would outgrow this. Though Wa Paw and her younger sister Paw Pa were to be baptized, their parents firmly expected to see them turn back to spirit worship as Mu Lay Moe and her sister had done a generation before. Wa Paw and Paw Pa, these two sisters, found themselves in the place of the ridiculed.

Ma Sing Way and her older sister, both of whom the village counted as immoral, were the only young people to be baptized who had what could be considered family support. Their mother, Mang Way Moe, had been drawn to the Lord for some time. Ever since her husband had been put to death by tribal justice she had come to the meetings, and she often stopped by to inquire about the Lord. She would be making her own decision and commitment to the Lord even as her daughters were being baptized. But though these two sisters faced no opposition within their own home, the judgment of the village hung over them and their entire household. The villagers expected them to go the way of their father. Karen history, told and retold beside flickering open fireplaces in mountain huts, revealed the pattern. A criminal left a sure inheritance to his family. His children and grandchildren would follow his crooked path. Ma Sing Way and Mang Way both experienced what it was to be condemned.

Moses' Mother was a poor widow and her testimony was ignored. Bay Law Moe and Bay Law Bpa, because of the stigma of sins long before committed and not even by themselves, were despised.

What a group we were! The rejected, ridiculed, condemned, discounted and despised.

On the Sunday of the baptism a crowd gathered at the side of the river. Our river was deep and silver with a sparkling purity, and the huge trees on either bank were the great umbrella-shaped rain trees with thick dark leaves that appeared almost black in their own deep shade. There the few Christians were gathered around Bill at the water's edge, and Maw Dta's widow and the two daughters who had been to Bible school in Burma were very much in evidence.

Mu Lay Moe told us that we must sing a verse and chorus of "O Happy Day" in between each baptism because that was the way it was done in Burma. My immediate reaction was, "Nuts! It doesn't say anywhere in the Bible that you have to sing 'O Happy Day' at every baptism." But before I could open my mouth I realized how childish that was. "O Happy Day" is a joyous song of praise, and at that moment I couldn't think of a more appropriate song for the occasion. And I saw that it was quite a good idea to be singing in between each baptism as the next one to be baptized picked a way down the river bank and into the water.

Baptism in a dimly lit baptistry in a lovely sanctuary is a beautiful and solemn picture. It is really quite different when a heathen village gathers together to be entertained by their friends who are going to come up out of the water with their clothes and hair streaming. But maybe the meaning of being identified with the One who was despised and rejected is more shockingly apparent. The ones to be baptized were not joining the "in group" as in a church ceremony. They were taking their place as outsiders and were already beginning to feel the stigma that our Lord bore all through His earthly life.

There were some hecklers who teased and called out as each one was baptized. There were others whose reactions were hidden behind the sloe-eyed, inscrutable Oriental mask. As they watched with unreadable expressions, I wondered what they were thinking and how they were drawn.

Just before Wa Paw's baptism I caught her father's eye. Yes, Mu Lay Bpa had been waiting to call out, "Did you see God?" I felt like a candle snuffer as I watched all the spark go out of him. Quelled by my eye, he subsided into sheepish silence.

After the baptism we were all to gather on my porch to observe communion. I longed that this time of remembering His death until He comes again would be a time when we could all be aware of His presence. But I was remembering what Bill and Rosemary had told me of the first time the Maesod congregation had observed communion. There, too, the communion was to follow the first baptism the church had ever seen. Bill had given clear teaching about the meaning behind the two services and had admonished the group to prepare themselves for the baptism and communion. When the congregation regathered in the little church building after the trip out to the river bordering Burma for the baptismal service, Rosemary took the tray of communion elements covered by a white cloth to a table at the front of the sanctuary. Having read the communion service from 1 Corinthians, Bill started to fold back the white cloth when he realized that the leading men in the group had all risen and were going out the back door. But then they came back with a crate of Pepsis and a plastic bag full of market cookies.

Admonished to prepare for the communion, Mai Lang and the other Christian men thought this meant that they must buy wine and bread. There were no grapes or wine available in Maesod, so the men felt perhaps Pepsis were close enough, and for bread they found the market cookies shaped like guns! This was a great favorite for the children as you can shoot all your friends with your cookie before you eat it. The awe-inspiring thing about that service is that Bill and Rosemary were able to act as if that were very ordinary and then were able to gather up the group and lead them into a quiet and solemn awareness of the Lord in their midst.

I did so hope that in our gathering together, just a tiny group, we would be aware of Him. I so hoped that His body broken for us would capture our full thoughts. I longed that His blood shed on the cross would assume importance in all our lives that would forever destroy the drawing attraction of those sins for which He suffered. But I knew that it was most unlikely that we would have the sacred atmosphere in which such a contemplation and awareness are possible.

There was Moses, a tiny and vocal baby, and though his older sister would take him down under the house, I knew that she was too small and too naughty to really keep him quiet. Mu Lay Moe had all her children in tow as did Bay Law Moe. Then Mang Way Moe, who was awaiting the next baptism, had decided to bring all her children to watch this part of the Christian worship. We could expect to have four babies all crying at once and several toddlers and older children trying to quiet them.

We did not own the lovely sort of communion sets that are used at home. I had thought of the type of service where one cup is shared by all. But Maw Dta's widow probably had tuberculosis, and I thought it just possible that Da Paw also had the disease. I knew that in their own homes they all used an unwashed cup to drink from the water jar on the front porch, and though I used those cups myself when staying in a Karen home, I did not feel that I should start a service of our Christian community that would follow this pattern. So we were using every glass I owned, and a few plastic coffee cups were added to make up the number needed. Two or three small juice glasses, four water glasses and a few plastic coffee cups did not make up an awe-inspiring array!

I knew that the juice we were using was grape Kool-aid and that the bread had been made from flour that was literally walking away with weevils. Though I had sifted out the actual bugs they had left their aroma and taste. I could hardly believe that the Karen were going to be able to see the eternal reality behind those symbols for there seemed nothing sacred, nothing venerable, nothing hallowed about that common tray of drink and bread.

But I had never been able to put myself in the place of a spirit-worshiping Karen who walks in dreadful fear and awe of the sacrifice bleeding in the hands of the spirit doctor. I did not know that just the reading of the familiar passage, "The Lord Jesus, the same night He was betrayed, took the bread; and when He had given thanks, He broke it and said, 'Take, eat, this is My body, which is broken for you; this do in remembrance of Me.' And after the same manner also He took the cup, when He had supped, saying, 'This cup is the new testament in My blood; this do, as often as ye drink it, in remembrance of Me,' " would send thrills of understanding through the group. Others have told me since of their first communion and its electrifying effect on them. They knew already that the Son of God had died for them, that He was the only acceptable sacrifice for their sins, and that in His death He reconciled them to the Father. But it was seeing the bread broken in the hands of the one leading the communion service, it was seeing the red liquid, that caused Calvary's bleeding sacrifice to become real to them. Then the ugly offense of spirit worship with its blasphemous counterfeit sacrifice became their greatest shame.

I had told the gospel stories and the parables of Christ. I had explained the picture charts and the flash cards, but it was the picture of communion about the broken bread and the cup that would get past ears that only wanted to be entertained and eyes that wanted to be charmed. The communion service was going to speak to hearts.

We were a pitiful and despised handful that made up the Maw Dta church family. But the testimony we had to give would not long be despised. God had started with influential men when He started the church in Maesod; in Maw Dta there was not one person of influence in that first group of believers. I'm sure if I had been asked my opinion about this at the time, I would have judged that we were falling far short of God's pattern for dynamic church growth. Experience would teach me what the book of Acts could have taught me, that God does not limit Himself to any one pattern when He plants a church.

In the next few months, how God would surprise me, doing what I never anticipated at all.

Chapter 9

In a Dark Room

How many people have dashed to a corner bus stop only to see their bus pulling away into traffic? How many have arrived out of breath at an airport to hear the loudspeaker announce the departure of their flight? The dejected passenger who has missed his ride is all too common a picture. "I missed my plane!" or "I missed my bus!" causes no surprise. But in all my life I have only known of one couple who had to say, "We missed our elephant."

The Charterses stayed with me for two weeks and were planning to return then to Maesod. A group of loggers coming down from the hills with their elephants would be passing our village on their way to the logging fields south of us. They were to come by way of the old washed-out logging road in the hills just beyond our village. It was only a fifteen-minute walk up to the road, and one of the men had promised the Charterses that if they could get themselves up to the road before the elephant train passed, they could ride most of the way to Maesod. The Charterses didn't make it in time and so ended up their visit with a long, long walk to Maesod.

Bill and Rosemary had arrived two weeks before on an elephant. As Karen houses are purposely built up elephant-high, it should have been simple for them to just step off the elephant onto the porch. At least that is Karen thinking, and it does seem to work for them. But Bill, while much more agile than the others of us who are reduced to elephant riding in this mission, chose for himself the most impossible place to alight. Heading for our storeroom window, he banged his head on the low rafters and slithered off the elephant's head to meet a barrage of large canisters of flour, lard and sugar. Conquering these with only minor wounds, he landed on a bamboo tray of onions and potatoes. This wasn't exactly a promising start to their visit. And a missed elephant rather marred the close of their visit. But the days in between were of tremendous importance to me and to Maw Dta. I surely appreciated Bill's willingness to perform our first baptismal service, but on a very personal level I greatly enjoyed having fellowship with other missionaries and doubtless bent their ears in my delight to be speaking English once again.

That taste of fellowship made it all the harder for me to accept the news a few weeks later that Massey would be leaving Maw Dta. Her children had been attending a Christian boarding school in north Thailand, but their personal problems had caused them, one after another, to drop out of school. Remembering their father's death and the talk in Maesod at the time when he was hunted in the jungle by the police, it is no wonder that the three children were deeply disturbed people. Massey felt that her first responsibility and commission from the Lord was to return to Maesod and make a home for her children.

Even with the tiny Christian community in Maw Dta, I'm not sure I could have been brave enough to remain in the Karen hills without Massey if it had not been for two things that happened almost immediately after oxcarts moved Massey and her belongings to Maesod.

Joeky de Wolf, a Dutch co-worker who had just completed her Thai language study, came to visit Maw Dta for a few weeks at the request of the field leader. Never before nor since has the Thailand field leader requested of a worker in one language group that they stay for any length of time on a station where their language study would be useless and they would hear an incomprehensible babble all day long. Joeky (pronounced "youkey") came not only in obedience but with a spirit of adventure that made me see anew the green, green, shady rain forests of our hills. I had grown so used to our river lapping nearby I hardly noticed it. The calls of monkeys and the music of bird songs from the trees hiding the village had grown common. Joeky, seeing it all as an adventure, opened my eyes again to what had become familiar. As a nurse, Joeky brought a good supply of medicine with her. But as the few Christians were all quite well just then, there was no demand for her medicines, for the spirit doctors served the needs of all others in our area.

Then came an invitation that I was to go with my guest to visit in Ma Blee Moe's house. Ma Blee, the little daughter of the household and great-granddaughter of Maw Dta, had been feverishly ill for several days. Her worried mother had come daily to visit with the sick child tied to her back. We could see that the little three-year-old was becoming more and more ill and weak until it was frightening and tremendously frustrating for Joeky not to be able to help. She was brought to us because she begged to come, and in her feverish discomfort her mother did not dare to cross her. But more than the irritation of her sickly daughter Ma Blee Moe feared the anger of the spirit doctors and would not dare to so much as give her daughter an aspirin.

As a happy, healthy, chubby little toddler, Ma Blee had wobbled around singing "Rock of Ages." Now she did not sing, but weary with pain and crying she begged to be brought to our house. And then one morning as it began to get on toward noon, I realized that Ma Blee had not come. "She is dying," we were told. All the men of the village who had power with the spirit world had gathered at her house to make sacrifices for her and to read the bones of the sacrifices.

The children of the village were subdued that morning, for though death so often came to the village it was a dreaded presence that robbed every activity and relationship of joy.

Maw Dta's eldest daughter, Day Zay, was the mother of Ma Blee Bpa (Ma Blee's father). Day Zay, along with Mu Lay Moe, had been to a Christian school in Burma. But I knew that the spirit ceremonies taking place in her son's home were not some fearful foreign thing to her. This was indeed her own spiritual home. It was the Christian school that had been foreign, and upon graduating she had put it behind her and turned to walk again in the dark way that her heart had never forsaken. Her only hope now was in the blood of the spirit sacrifice draining away in the hands of the spirit doctor.

So often that was the story in Maw Dta. Pain and suffering and death with never a hope except in the blood of a sacrifice. As the blood of a pig or chicken drained away in the priest's hands, he desperately muttered his incantations while life and hope drained away before his eyes. But during those days when Joeky was with me, there was medicine and all her medical knowledge available to any who would receive it. Though the years of disappointment and sorrow had defeated and broken the spirits of the men who served the dark lords, they dared not let the people go free to try our medicine — for they themselves were gripped in a hand that would not give them the liberty to release those they held.

Grandfather Sickly once sent for Joeky. His problem was a great infected sore on his leg. Sores and cuts and infected insect bites are just too common to take to the spirit doctors who would not want to be bothered. Before the sore could be cleaned and medicine and bandage put on, Grandfather Sickly had to give us his very serious diagnosis of his most profound case.

"You know that man who died in Pa Gu Der's house last week? Well, it was a putrid wasting cough that ate all his innards that killed him! Before he died he vomited up all that was left of his lungs. He was all rotten before he died and was just an empty shell at his death. And it's the smell of that rotten dead man that is attacking my leg!"

Grandfather Sickly had whispered this diagnosis and now sat back to watch me translate it for Joeky. Surely her treatment would be influenced by his most expert diagnosis.

Because his little black eyes darted back and forth studying our expressions as I translated, we tried to look duly impressed.

But it was almost the end of my composure when Joeky had me tell him that he was indeed fortunate that the smell of the rotten dead man was attacking his leg and not his nose! This thought had escaped Grandfather Sickly's notice, and he was greatly impressed with Joeky. She was not only a healer of no mean ability but she was obviously a woman of great perception.

Though an ulcerated sore caused Grandfather Sickly to call for Joeky, never had I been called on to treat the fevers that killed our villagers. Then word came that we had been summoned to the house where Ma Blee was dying, and I could not imagine what this must mean.

At the foot of the steep bamboo ladder leading up to the one-room house was the familiar forked branch. The few leaves were already dry and turning brown at the edges. This was the sign that the spirit doctors were in the house and no outsider could enter. My questioning glance was answered by the reassurance that, having been summoned, we could ignore the sign of the branch.

For all Karen in our area tied to the ancient forms of spirit worship, the pattern of their house was alike. One room of bamboo served as kitchen, dining room and bedroom. A clay and ash platform three or four inches high, where a fire was kept burning most of the time, divided the room into a U-shape. Wind blowing through the loose weave of the bamboo kept ashes scattered about the room. Water carried into the house in bamboo joints strung from the head by a rattan strap was usually sloshed and spilled until the bamboo floor was tracked and muddy. Rice would be eaten while sitting on the floor, and if dogs or cats did not get every grain dropped by children's fingers then ants and cockroaches would invade often at night when the same floor space became bed for the household.

As we came in, then, out of the blinding light of a tropical noonday, the little one-room house seemed an empty black hole. Joeky and I quickly sat down just inside the door. We hardly dared to try to cross that black room. As our eyes began to adjust to the blackness we could see that a mat had been laid out in the center of the room, and the dying child was convulsed there with a spirit doctor bending over her. About the walls of the room sat the other men who were acting as spirit doctors.

Until that day I had never seen a Karen man dressed in the long red homespun priest's robe. For a generation or more the robes had been worn only for sacrifices and secret ceremonies. Donned over more conventional dress within the privacy of home or secluded sacred spot, the garment would be removed before any outsider could see it. Once the long red robe had been the only dress for Karen men, but contact with the outside world brought the men of the tribe to adopt Western and Thai styles. But as with all traditional Karen dress, not only the design but also every step in the process from spinning thread to the last bit of weaving was governed by rules of spirit worship. As the virgins' white dress was required for a heathen funeral, the men's red robe was required for spirit ceremonies. When the ceremonies were finished the priest would emerge, his robes were put away, and he was again a farmer, logger or craftsman.

Now seated on the inside at a spirit ceremony, I saw the men of my village as priests. Their red robes were almost black in the gloom, and if it had not been for the whites of their eyes I could have doubted that they were there at all. Almost without looking, I knew who they were.

And though I could not bear to look at the child convulsing there with just her head and heels touching the mat, neither did I want to see that head spirit doctor working over her. I did not want to see those other men either. I did not want to see them like that, as spirit doctors, these men of the village that I knew as fathers and hard-working farmers. I wanted to be able to go on thinking of them as kindly men who loved their families and cared for their friends and neighbors. I did not want to have that picture of them overlaid with this new revelation of them as men who had sought to know and have power with the evil spirit world.

Now they wore the red robes of the priesthood and since early morning had been drinking and chanting. Designs had been drawn on the floor, a sacrifice had been killed, and incantations had been made. At last the bones of the sacrifice had been read and hope was all gone, for the message was that the child would die.

I could not read any emotion on the face of the head spirit doctor. But I was overcome with my own emotional reaction as I realized who he was: Mu Lay Bpa.

It would be months later before I would hear his story and learn of the heavy burden that, with the threatened death of his own niece, had become more than he could carry. For days he had tried every cure known to the doctors. One cure that was tried had almost seemed to work. This was a mixture that was spread all over the suffering baby. I could hardly believe my ears when I was told of the ingredients of that mixture, but I had to believe my eyes — and the proof was right there for me to see in my own home.

We had an all-black cat with no markings. Eustace was a lazy tomcat who would catch a mouse only if it was dead, cooked, and served with his rice. So I was most surprised when neighbors of Ma Blee Moe came to ask if they could borrow Eustace to catch rats in their home. The next day Eustace was returned to us minus one ear. We were told most apologetically that Eustace had got into a fight with a dog of the household. We were never tempted to believe that — unless the dog was most adept with a knife — for it was plain to see that the ear had been cleanly cut away. We never imagined the truth, however. The ancient spirit cure called for the left ear of an all-black cat. When one of the children told us of this, Joeky's response was that we should be glad that the cure had not called for the right ear of a white woman!

That cure and every other one tried by the spirit doctors had ended in failure. It was obvious that the little child arched there in convulsions in that dark room was at the edge of the grave. I could not help but feel the horror and sorrow of death, and yet I knew that the child was not going from life into death but rather from death into life. That room, that village, and all our mountain world were held in the grip of death.

Mu Lay Bpa asked if Joeky as a nurse could do anything for Ma Blee and I translated his question for her. Joeky answered that the penicillin she had was slow acting and she feared that the child would die before an injection could begin to act. Nevertheless, she surely was willing to give the injection if the men were willing for it. Mu Lay Bpa's eyes shifted their concentration from Joeky's face as she spoke to study me as I translated what she had been speaking.

I hardly dared to hope that the spirit doctors would allow the injection to be given. What if the child died just as the needle pierced the skin? There would be those who would say that Joeky had killed Ma Blee.

Joeky and I knew that God can heal. We had no doubts about His power, but we had nothing but doubts about His pleasure in this particular situation. We dared not try to commit Him to a course of action. It would have been the height of presumption for us to make a judgment that in this case God ought to heal or surely would want to heal.

We were guests in the dark room, allowed just inside the door. We were asked one question, allowed to answer, and then given permission to leave.

The men exchanged glances and nods were given around the circle. Mu Lay Bpa again answered for all. Yes, they wanted the injection. We hurried from that house for Joeky to prepare her syringe. But even before we could build a charcoal fire to boil the syringes we heard the funeral wail echo up through the village. Ma Blee was dead!

Joeky and I were stunned. I had not known what to expect God to do, but I surely was not expecting this news of Ma Blee's death. With the horrifying death wail sounding all around I longed to see this circumstance from God's perspective, and to understand what He was planning and why He allowed this child to die. I judged that God was on trial before this village and it seemed to me that He had chosen once again to allow men to despise Him, esteem Him as nothing; at this moment of power confrontation He had veiled His power and Person and chose not to be seen by an unbelieving village.

That shows just how wrong I can be! God chose to speak to Maw Dta with a still, small voice. In hills where demonic powers have raged for centuries as fire out of control, destructive whirlwinds and terrifying storms, God chose to move silently, gently, in a dark room where spirit doctors had come to the end of what they could endure.

They made a choice before Joeky and I ever stepped into that room of darkness. The spirit doctors denied the sacred way by allowing us to climb the stairs when the forked branch was in place. We should never have been allowed to see those men in their robes or the designs on the floor or the markings on the child's body. (The truth is, we never did see those things, for we were not there long enough for our eyes to adjust to the darkness. But the men who sent for us did not realize this.) In the minds of the spirit doctors they were exposing their secret way to us.

They had chosen to offend their masters and had put themselves in great danger. There was only one reason for their decision. They had for years been hearing stories and teachings of Jesus Christ, and bit by bit, understanding and longing were born in the hearts of some. It was that divine restlessness and longing that now forced them to move. But God was going to hold them to a response of faith in His Word. He did not choose that His church should be built on a miracle of healing.

Every pattern and part of spirit worship in the Karen hills is built on a miracle and a personality. Men who were held in the haunting bondage of fear of the unseen around them were willing to live in tiny isolated villages simply because there was in every village a strong spirit doctor who could inspire a sense of security and protection because he could manipulate the spirits. Accounts of miraculous healings were always a part of such a man's verification that he was a spirit doctor. God was not going to parallel that sort of movement. There would be no outward show to appeal to the senses; there would be no human personality to draw the hearts of the people. The Karen converts would come through the narrow way of faith in the death and resurrection of Jesus Christ. The only miracle they would then see was the power of His resurrection life working in them.

To my complete surprise those spirit doctors came then, one and two at a time, to tell of their decision to turn from the dark worship of evil spirits to the God of creation, the Lord of salvation, the Holy God of eternity.

Mu Lay Bpa, the head spirit doctor, spent days wrestling with the Lord. During his visits with me in the days after Ma Blee died, it was obvious that he was a man pulled in two directions. He knew all the rules as long as he stayed a spirit doctor. He knew that if he were to become a Christian he would be behind even his own children in his understanding of this new way. It would be for him an experience of becoming as a little child. He wouldn't know the answers and he would have no place of importance. As a spirit doctor he was a powerful voice; as a Christian he could only raise his voice to ask questions.

In his frustration, one day Mu Lay Bpa set out for his hill field alone. Alone he climbed the steep hill that overshadowed our village. The top of the hill was covered in a white mist and he remarked to himself, as Karen often do, "Go La Joe is wearing her head turban." (That white turban of clouds means there will shortly be a downpour.) Soon the threatening rain began to fall, and he wrapped himself in his piece of bright red plastic. Then, turning his crooked pipe upside down so the gusts of wind and rain wouldn't put it out, he trudged on up the steep path. He was just a small, miserable speck against the mountainside, fighting against the weather and the God of the weather. His land wasn't mapped, his people weren't counted, his family was not valued by the governments of this world. But the God of eternity had mapped out a strategy of reaching all of Mu Lay Bpa's family. God had even counted them in Christ before the foundation of the world, and He was pursuing Mu Lay Bpa's steps up the side of Go La Joe.

Alone, there on that stormy mountainside, this spirit doctor whose hands were soiled with the blood of countless sacrifices suddenly saw the death of our Lord as the one sacrifice that secured forever the salvation of those who come to Him in faith. And seeing, he was already committed. He would sit in the congregation at the feet of the younger men and even women, willing to be a disciple along with those who once called him "thra" (teacher).

Because his eyes were damaged he would never learn to read. When he led in prayer his own daughters would correct him because he used the tones and language of a spirit doctor. It was his own daughters who taught him to pray, admonishing, "Just talk to God; don't sing at Him!"

But Mu Lay Bpa would accept the position of a lowly disciple without struggle. With conversion he left behind the desire to be important, and in his humility God would make him a more important voice than he had ever been before.

With his village, Mu Lay Bpa was moving out of the intense darkness of the lost into the glorious light of salvation.

Joeky's visit came just at the time when I was feeling that I simply couldn't go on living in Maw Dta without a co-worker and without Massey. And Joeky's visit extended into that wave of conversions which followed Ma Blee's death. I will be honest and admit that before Joeky's visit I was feeling sorry for myself that I had to live alone in a Karen village. But with that wave of conversions following Ma Blee's death, I could never look back. I would never again be tempted to feel sorry for myself, that I had to be isolated in such a place. For I then realized that I was one of the richest people in all the world: I was receiving from God a treasure, a tremendous harvest, a harvest I could never have earned.

Chapter 10

Seven More to Feed

As the Lord kept adding to the Christian community, I kept wondering when someone would notice that I was not adequate for the work I had to do. Though there were more than thirty missionaries with WEC in Thailand in those days, apart from the Peterses who were settled in their distant village no one else felt God calling them to work with the Karen. So I was responsible for the missionary operation in the Maw Dta area, an area that could only be ministered to on foot or by elephant. Even for a swift Karen walker it could not be covered in less than two weeks from north to south, or in three days from east to west.

Not only was I inadequate to reach the vast unevangelized area, but the tiny area I had penetrated with the gospel was magnifying another problem. I was disorganized. Sunday morning meetings started when a few people had gathered. Others, hearing the singing, hurried to finish breakfast in order to join us. And some, coming across the fields from a village named for their headman Cad Way, arrived so late that we had to have a second meeting for them. This second meeting was never because we were such a large crowd, but because we were just so disorganized that I could not keep the first meeting from starting until all had gathered. In fact, I often left my own breakfast unfinished because the singing had started on either my porch or someone else's.

Sunday evening meetings I thought of as adult Sunday

School, when I used flash cards and picture rolls and any other help I could find for teaching Bible stories. In my own mind I felt that the evening meeting could be more relaxed and informal than the morning worship service. The only trouble was that the morning meetings themselves at times turned into an open conversation, with questions, answers, testimonies, praise, and prayer requests; it was impossible for any meeting to be more informal than our morning worship service!

It is the perfect example of my muddled disorder that in a few months we had outgrown every available porch in the village and were in critical need of a building that could accommodate us, and yet I had completely forgotten ever to take an offering! Nor had I ever taught anything about Christian giving.

I should say in my own defense that I was awed by the generosity of my Christian neighbors, who often received guests from the hills coming to observe Christian worship. I noted that guests were fed royally, and Monday when they departed the host family would often be left without so much as a grain of rice. Some trade would have to be carried out or some debt collected before that family could eat their next meal. This generosity within the growing Christian family was a giving in love and in joy, and it was a great blessing for me to watch.

Eventually the fact that we had need of a building but had no church treasury brought us to a crisis. When it all was discussed at a very crowded porch meeting, headman Cad Way told me he would take charge of ordering materials for a small bamboo structure that would just accommodate us, and we would start taking offerings with the building of a more permanent structure in mind.

In my ignorance I assumed Cad Way would encourage the Christians to work together cutting bamboo and splitting it for flooring, and that different households would contribute for the roofing their extra leaves that had been strung on thin bamboo strips. When the building was erected — one that would seat comfortably about fifty (that is, if you can sit

(1) *The first bamboo church in Maw Dta.*
(2) *Baptism in our own river.*

comfortably on the floor) — it came as a great shock to me to hear Cad Way read off the names and amounts of money given by donors for the building. He had gone with paper and pencil to every house in our village and his own across the rice fields from us, asking for donations! It was my fault, of course, for I had not taught the Christian privilege of giving or the discipline of trusting the Lord to supply through His people as He would prompt them.

Almost half of the gifts of money that were given for that first Maw Dta church building came from the unsaved! I'm sure that some of those who contributed gave out of respect for the headman who was collecting. Others were fearful of refusing so important a man. In the world of business and politics this would have been labeled bribery and corruption. Another group of donors was those whose contacts with Thai Buddhists had conditioned them to think in terms of making merit. Their gifts would be thought of as balancing against the sins registered to their account. In the building of that first little meetinghouse we surely missed the privilege that Christians have of expressing their love for the Lord in building a house of worship. It all taught me a lesson and I determined that never again would any group I worked with miss that blessing.

As the Maw Dta congregation grew week by week, the hills were beginning to respond and ask for someone to come and explain the meaning of this new way to them.

By the time our bamboo church was completed there was a string of responsive villages that stretched up the valley between the hills and into the mountain pass, each with one or more Christian households to be visited and taught and encouraged. Maw Dta and Cad Way's village were really a full-time job, because the new believers had to be taught to read and write before they could go very far in understanding this new way. Yet it did not appear that God was going to send any others to help in this ministry.

Then they came — from Burma.

I had understood that Maw Dta's Christian relatives from Burma never visited Thailand. Now word came that a group was coming to have a memorial service for headman Maw Dta.

Two Christian boys came first to tell us of the proposed visit. There would be a choir made up of the best singers from several small congregations. There also would be at least six pastors. This was to be a joint project of several churches and they called it an evangelistic campaign. I was delighted that they were coming and felt that the chance for our folk to have fellowship with older Karen Christians was going to be of great value. However, I was a bit confused. None of the Christian communities represented by the choir members and pastors was as far away from Maw Dta as was Maesod! I would have expected them to have made Maw Dta a target of evangelism twenty years before. Why had Maw Dta asked Wilf Overgaard to send someone to teach his people about the Lord when he could have sent that request to one of these Karen pastors?

"We couldn't have come across before," the two boys explained. It was then that I heard of that long-ago response that the church of Burma had sent, saying they would not sow among thorns.

It seems that the Thai hill people had such bad reputations that none of the Karen Christians from Burma had been willing to venture into this deadly territory until Mu Lay Bpa and the new headman for our village, Pa Gu Der, a grandson-in-law of Maw Dta, had gone to visit over there and had told how they had become Christians. Now that there was a fellowship of believers it was safe for the convention of churches across the border to make us the object of their evangelistic outreach. I thought the two forerunners of the campaign must be a bit weak in vocabulary. They surely were using "evangelism" in the wrong way and meant "fellowship." After all, you don't evangelize Christians!

With all the Christians and all of the Maw Dta family we prepared for the coming of the campaign. And it was great. The Karen from Burma walked in through the pathless rain forests from the border a two-hour walk away. There were more than twenty young people and a dozen adults with guitars, banjos and mandolins. That choir of twenty sounded like a hundred voices, and Maw Dta was overwhelmed.

The memorial service for Grandfather Maw Dta was held beside his grave. The grave plot had been marked by a simple white cross under the shade of flowering frangipani trees with the heady scent of jasmine perfuming the air. I had always felt that this unpretentious grave was a dramatic invasion. This grave, in the midst of a people who never wanted to be reminded of the dead and never marked a burial spot, was a loud and powerful testimony.

The two forerunners of the campaign had been given instructions to fix up the grave site. They had bought bricks from the closest Thai village and built something that, when painted white, looked like a huge coffin above the ground. It was such an imposing sight that I felt it could only be called a sarcophagus. The village thought this monstrosity was absolutely marvelous, while I felt the simple cross under the blossoming shade trees had had a quiet and compelling dignity. But I kept my thoughts to myself.

The memorial service was really very fitting for it was right that the memory of that tiny man should be so honored. Over half a lifetime he had stood alone, the only one in all his land who chose to worship God.

The entire village attended the service, sitting on woven bamboo mats spread under the flowering trees. My chairs had been borrowed for the visiting dignitaries and I was given a place among them, and asked to give a word of tribute to Maw Dta, though the men from Burma despised my Karen speech; I had discarded the rules and vocabulary learned from the Burmese university-level language study course to adapt to the speech habits of the hill people of Thailand. The obvious scorn of the visiting pastors for my hillbilly language sent me home after the meeting discouraged and needing to seek the Lord's mind. But once more I knew in my heart that the Lord was requiring me to communicate the gospel, and I must not obscure it by vocabulary and grammar rules unfamiliar to the hill people. After all, the Lord had not sent me to evangelize the highly educated few of Burma's Karen elite; He had sent me to reach the thousands of untaught, untold Karen of Thailand's hills. I must speak as they spoke, or they would not understand.

The next Sunday the group from Burma was still to be in the village and they would worship with us in our little bamboo building. The six pastors sent word to me that they would be happy to baptize any who wanted to be baptized. They would lead a communion service, and they would have a dedication service for our new church building.

A missionary couple, Jim and Emma Mitchell, had started a work in Maeramard, a Thai town about five hours' walk from Maw Dta. Jim was willing to come and perform baptismal services for us every few weeks. And though we had had a baptismal service scarcely a month before this visit from Burma, there were again eight Christians ready for baptism.

I was not comfortable when I found that to the eight folk that the Maw Dta Christian family considered ready for baptism the pastors from Burma had added another five. The eight had been meeting with us for some weeks and had counted themselves as followers of the Lord's way. The five new ones added by the pastors had never before made any claim to faith nor expressed any desire to be part of the Christian family. The worship service on the morning of their baptism would be the first time they had come openly to meet with God's people. I was definitely unhappy about this, but I met with a wall that I could not in any way penetrate. These men from Burma were older, established pastors, and they would do as they chose. Since none of the Maw Dta believers had been saved for any length of time, except for the youngsters, we were without any lay leadership that might have had influence on these men from Burma. So along with the eight I knew to be following the Lord would be these five others whose profession of faith they themselves had never had the chance to test. Was their baptism a testimony of faith or a response of admiration and honor for our visitors?

The church service was all any evangelical Christian could desire. Keddy, the young pastor who spoke, really impressed me. I felt that his message could have come from the pulpit of one of the great Bible-teaching churches of the West. This was a young man who knew how to feed the sheep, and I thought to myself that if the five extra who were to be baptized at the end of the service really listened and received, they could go down into the waters of baptism truly experiencing faith.

In the afternoon, after all the services were over, a delegation of the six pastors came to confer with me. They asked if I would accept one who came with them who felt called to work in Thailand. It was their desire that he join me in the work in the Maw Dta area. His name was Pa Low.

Pa Low was a Bible school graduate of many years before. He and his wife had formerly lived in Thailand for several years, and independent of any sponsorship they had sought to serve the Lord. But their village had been attacked by robbers again and again, and there had been no response there to Pa Low's message. At last, with his wife broken in health and very depressed because of the death of their eldest son, they had returned to Burma. However, they had never been settled, and they felt that they were turning their backs on the call of the Lord. So now, with the encouragement of these pastors from Burma, Pa Low with his wife and three sons was looking again to Thailand and hoping to join me in the Maw Dta work.

While the delegation from Burma was with us Pa Low had been visiting with the Christian families, and everyone was enthusiastic about the prospect of his moving in with his family to become a part of our evangelistic outreach. It seemed so right that Pa Low should come to join me and help out in this work of harvesting the Karen hills.

As a Karen, he immediately understood that it was unacceptable in their culture for me as a woman to expect hospitality where I had not been invited. I therefore could not evangelize in the hills. In our talking together, he agreed that he would take on that job. The interest of the hills in the growing Christian community would be an open door for him and he could travel, telling what the Christians had come to believe. He told me that he had relatives to the northeast of us, and he would want to visit them as he hoped to win them to the Lord. He was also still very concerned for the village where he had once lived.

During our conversation that day I saw that on basic doctrines we were agreed, and that our burden for the lost was the same. Surely method and strategy we would be able to work out in time.

I did have the passing thought that I wished it were Keddy, the outstanding preacher, that God was calling to work in Maw Dta. But I was told that Keddy would soon take on the position of principal in a Christian school in south Burma.

I thought at the time that the only real problem was money. Pa Low wanted to be a full-time Christian worker and the Maw Dta believers expected this of him. But our weekly offerings wouldn't begin to feed and clothe a family of five. Our WEC field policy was that as a mission we did not pay national workers. There were many reasons for this. Perhaps the main reason was our commitment to indigenous principles. We believe the local church is a fellowship of believers who build their own place of worship and support their own outreach and teaching ministries. As missionaries we did not expect to govern or completely support any work or individual pastor or evangelist.

Though we did not as a mission offer employment, we were free as individuals to give as we felt led to the Lord's work. Consequently, many missionaries helped young Thai Christians to go to Bible school or contributed to the support of national workers. But this liberty to use my personal money to help Pa Low was really not much of a help to me, for I seldom had any personal money.

WEC's financial policy is very simple. Every missionary is to look to God alone for support and the supply of all his or her needs. No one in WEC is ever to state from a public platform that they need money for support, travel or outfit. No prayer letter is ever to be sent asking for financial aid or to list needs. Finances are not to be mentioned except in positive testimony and praise of God's provisions.

There is no set amount of money that candidates have to raise for their monthly support before they can set out for the land of their work. But candidates are told what the average amount needed to live on a modest scale in their adopted country will be so they can be asking the Lord for His supply. WEC missionaries certainly ask for money. They just never ask the people of God; instead they go to the top and ask the God of His people. And He does move His people to give. When an accepted candidate has what is necessary to pay the passage to his country, he is free to go even though he may not have even one penny of promised support!

As a young person in Bible school this financial policy seemed frightening and daring. Yet at the same time it attracted and challenged me. I felt certain that God was leading me to apply to WEC, and that meant that WEC's faith policy must become mine.

I sailed for Thailand the first time with just ten dollars a month promised support. So the fact that all my needs were met month by month stamped me indelibly with the assurance that my support was God's business and He would provide.

I knew those who sent regularly for my support were not just thinking of keeping me fed and clothed and housed; they were giving *through me* to a needy people. Gifts and support sent to me passed on through me to meet again and again the needs of the hungry, the unclothed, and the ill.

Now would God supply through me the needs of national workers? My spontaneous answer had to be yes. But only if national workers supported by foreign funds were God's answer to the need of the Karen hills. So it was with a feeling that I was stepping on very shaky ground that I promised to share with the Pa Low family what I received, for I was not at all certain that nationals supported by foreign funds was God's way for us. I knew full well that if the Lord was not in this we would all be learning a great deal about hunger in the next few months! The church wanted Pa Low; it would have been so much more simple if the church could have supported him.

It was almost a year between my agreeing to work with Pa

Low and the day he arrived in Maw Dta, bringing his family with him. In the meantime another young man came from Burma requesting to work with me. Though he was even better qualified than Pa Low and seemed to capture the hearts of the Christians, I did not dare to give him any encouragement. Johnson went back to Burma after just one weekend in Maw Dta, looking absolutely miserable. The Christian fellowship of Maw Dta seemed so disappointed that I felt I had betrayed the Lord in not being able to rise in faith and promise Johnson support.

In time, Pa Low arrived with his family, and many of his friends from Burma came along, helping them carry their belongings. Not many days after, Keddy, the young man who had so impressed me as an outstanding speaker, arrived. His job as principal of a Christian school had fallen through and he announced that he too had come to serve the Karen church in Thailand. Though he did not mention support it was obvious that he was going to need financial help. Keddy had come from Burma in the rainy season, and had had to swim the Mooie River that forms our border; it is usually shallow, but the monsoon rains had made it treacherous to cross during that season. So he had only the clothes he stood in and a waterproof shoulder bag that held little more than a few books.

A few days later I arrived home from an elephant trip to hear that Johnson had come again, expecting to work in Maw Dta. I really wondered if something had happened to my hearing. This just couldn't be true!

Riding along that morning, my elephant boy who rejoiced in a name meaning "Dirty" had forced the elephant against her will to venture onto a rickety bridge. The elephant's foot had gone right through a rotten board and she fell heavily onto her chest or chin. (I am not too clear on elephant anatomy.) I fell off over her head, but was not at all hurt because as I fell I knocked Dirty off and absolutely squashed him in a shallow mud puddle. The most alarming thing at the time had been that the poor elephant, reaching around for the sturdiest thing she could find to hang onto, had wrapped her trunk around my leg! I concluded at the time that I had escaped unhurt, and was not even badly shaken up. But when I arrived home that afternoon to be told that I had inherited yet another worker to support, I sat there in a daze, fanning myself with my rubber flip-flop shoe (so I was told!). And I really wondered if perhaps I would wake up in the hospital to find my head permanently damaged by that fall. *Another worker!* — that just could not be true. Pa Low, with a family of five, Keddy and now Johnson, all needing support! — it was too unreal.

"Lord, You have sent me seven mouths to feed and now I expect You to send the food," I told Him that night. And one earmark of the next few months was that the Lord did just that. Money was no problem.

I cannot doubt that God was in the plan for me to help those men, for He supplied through me all that we needed. But looking back over the years I can see that God allowed that venture so as to corner me into a plan of church expansion that did not rest on the services of full-time paid workers. There was something quite different that God was planning to do in this corner of His world. He would let me use clergy first, and then He would show me what He had chosen for Maw Dta.

Chapter 11

Presenting the Gospel or Presenting a Community?

It is basic to Karen thinking that men should take leadership in everything that is truly important. The reaching of the whole tribe with the gospel was now the most important thing in the world to several Christian families, so they welcomed Pa Low (as they would the other two workers who showed up) with every intention of following his lead and helping him in every way they possibly could.

The men of the Maw Dta church gave and prepared all the materials necessary to build a bamboo house for Pa Low and his family: house posts and poles for the frame, flattened bamboo for the walls and floor, and leaves strung on long sticks for the roofing. Everyone gave so generously that by the time the materials for the house were completed the family had all they needed to furnish the house on a simple Karen standard. During this time when the materials were being gathered and prepared, a period lasting about a month, he and his family lived with me in my home. Pa Low was not well during that time and so did not help at all with the work that was done in preparation for his family's house.

The Karen of Maw Dta were being helpful in every way they knew how, but they were also watching and they were seeing and remembering things that I was not noticing at all. In that month the church attitude toward Pa Low was changing completely, and I did not know it.

Pa Low's illness was one that I was hearing about all the time, and I just couldn't understand it. He had "cold hands and feet"! And this fearful complaint totally disabled him! This sounded bizarre to me and I thought, "There must be some more-understandable symptoms that he is not telling me about."

I was slowly learning that the Karen way of describing the symptoms of illness was perhaps the most extraordinary thing about them. A "salty throat" is the first symptom of a cold. To say that "the world is becoming freckled" is the Karen way of expressing dizziness. What fearful disease could "cold hands and feet" signify?

Though I could not understand what Pa Low's symptoms might mean, I believed that he was truly ill and I blamed his illness for the fact that he did not help at all in preparing the bamboo materials for his house. The Karen agreed that cold hands and feet were the symptoms of misery, but they felt he should be helping and began to resent that he would use them as unpaid servants.

I was much later to understand that just across the border from us pastors actually referred to their congregations as their "servants." Had the congregations called the pastors their servants, I could have felt quite comfortable with that. But I found their concept exactly the opposite of mine. I had felt that I was in Maw Dta to serve the Karen and I had expected that men called to the Lord's work would feel the same. In Mark's Gospel the Lord speaks in 10:43 about those who would be called "minister," and moves on in the next verse to say that these should be "the servant of all." I would never, from Burma, meet the attitude that the Lord's servant is the servant of the Lord's people.

I did not realize, during those days when Pa Low's house was being prepared, that the men of Maw Dta were looking for an attitude of heart that would make Pa Low get down beside them and work with them. If Pa Low had been a woman who could not build a house, that would have been different; but the men of Maw Dta knew that he had built a dozen or more bamboo houses over the years. They felt he was elevating himself to a position of importance because he would not now help with preparing materials for his house. They were slowly coming to the conclusion that they did not want him in authority over them.

During the month or so that Pa Low's family lived in my house, I was going out most mornings to teach reading to a group of young people in Thaw Ray Blaw, a village an hour's walk away. Since none of Pa Low's three boys could read, they followed along to be a part of those classes. With the girls who lived with me and a few of their friends, some stray dogs and Pa Low's boys, we would start off early each morning and return about noon. I knew that in our absence the men of Maw Dta were visiting Pa Low and drinking endless cups of Burmese tea and eating slabs of brown sugar. I trusted that in their talking together they would experience a mutual blessing.

I was quite shocked, then, when I learned that the Christian men each spent only one day in the actual erecting of Pa Low's house. That is the custom that operates between casual friends; one day's help is expected of every neighbor. A bamboo house is almost finished after that one day of actual building, but a man's close friends and relatives will help him until all is finished.

It was quite obvious that if all the church family helped a second day, the house would have been completed. Christians were helping each other all the time, giving a second day's labor. It had become standard practice for Christian brothers to help each other till any Christian's house was finished, but they were not going to help Pa Low beyond one day. In helping just that one day they were establishing that none of them were close, intimate friends or family, but I could not discern where the offense had been given.

Eventually Pa Low got up off his sickbed and finished his house all by himself. I sensed that he was judging the Maw Dta believers to be pretty poor specimens of Christianity in that they would not help him, and by that time I realized that the Maw Dta Christians were also harshly judging him.

Cold hands and cold feet were spoken of among the Karen as being a miserable complaint. But men and women with the same complaint went right on with their field work. Carrying heavy burdens and building houses, planting and harvesting —all had to be done. And a Karen just had to endure cold hands and cold feet. I was later told that these were the symptoms of vitamin B deficiency. Since I treated almost all illnesses with vitamins and iron in those days, I'm sure Pa Low did get the medicine he needed. But I was in no position to judge. Perhaps he was unable to assimilate the vitamins in the form in which they were given.

I am no administrator and did not tell Pa Low what to do. Instead, he told me what he wanted to do. His taking responsibility for the evangelistic outreach to the hills, where I could not go, sounded great.

With his house finished, Pa Low visited the area where he and his family had once lived. He visited his scattered relatives and contacts he had had from his stay in Thailand years before. But he was not encouraged. I then urged him to visit hill villages where there were Christian households, for as the church grew in Maw Dta, relatives and friends of the new converts scattered in the hills were aroused to interest. And where we fed that interest with the simple account of who Jesus Christ was and what He did, that interest became faith.

As I watched Pa Low trudge up the path out of our village for those hill visits, however, I became deeply disturbed that none of the Christian men accompanied him. These were visits to their friends and family. Did they not want to be part of the witness that would bring salvation to those they knew and loved? I urged Pa Low to invite the men of Maw Dta to go with him, and I tried to challenge them to go, but I was meeting a definite resistance. Though answers were evasive, every answer was no!

I also encouraged Pa Low to visit Bob and Alice Peters in their area. Bob wanted Pa Low to go on trek with him through unevangelized villages and I was so thankful for this, for I was beginning to wonder if Pa Low didn't perhaps need to be under the leadership of a man. But when he returned from the Peterses', I could see that Pa Low was not heartened and seemed dissatisfied with the way our mission worked in Thailand.

I had given Pa Low no supervision at first. But during those days when his family lived with me and we talked much of what we hoped to see accomplished, and prayed together for the spread of the church in Thailand, he must have been appalled as he got the picture of what I was expecting of him. It was not until years later that I grasped what his idea of evangelism was and began to see how I must have upset and bewildered him.

I should have recalled the memorial service of the year before. I had then thought that the young men who spoke of their memorial service for Maw Dta as an "evangelistic campaign" were using the wrong words, for I thought of their visit to us in terms of fellowship and of encouragement by older believers for a new Christian community. But they meant just what they said. In Burma where the church has long existed side by side with spirit worship, Christian outreach is a community project. A church community thinks in terms of an annual campaign of two or three days' visit to some target village where there would be some Christian homes to give them hospitality. The visitors then add their corporate testimony to that of their hosts, in programs for the unsaved of the community.

I realize, looking back, that Pa Low had no idea of going alone, or even with a companion, to villages where there were no Christians; reaching into the black pit of spirit worship and bringing light just by opening the Scriptures was a concept foreign to him. Coming from Burma, Pa Low thought in terms of what *they* would call evangelistic campaigns. He must have felt that Maw Dta, with its large young people's group, could form a choir, put on a concert and skits, and by the attractiveness of Christian community draw the unevangelized to them. Presenting the attractiveness of Christian community was to him the only way to evangelize.

He could see from conversation with me that I expected

him to go with a message. And though I expressed the hope that some of the Christian men would go with him from time to time, none of them had known the Lord for longer than two years — so he, of course, would be the one to be the Lord's mouthpiece.

To put it as simply as I know how, in my idea of evangelism all that is necessary is an open mouth speaking from an open Bible to at least one pair of open ears. To Pa Low, nothing less than a community endeavor could be thought of as true evangelism.

While he was appalled at my concept of evangelism, I believe that at first Pa Low still had some hopes of doing it his way. But with the coming of Keddy and Johnson, who began to organize programs for the youth of Maw Dta, Pa Low found that as a much older man the youth were not so responsive to him. Had he explained his vision to me I probably would have urged the young people to go and do what he wanted, at least to one hill village where there were several Christian households and where I know that feeding such an invasion would not have imposed an unwelcome burden. But I never had any understanding of his frustration. I would never have thought of a campaign as being the method to use in reaching spirit-worshiping hill people for the Lord.

Pa Low never told me of his vision nor asked that the young people go campaigning, and I think that that is perhaps because as he visited the places he hoped to evangelize with a campaign he realized that there was in most places not even one home which would want or could afford to receive a big group. In expecting him to evangelize areas where there was not even one Christian, I was closing the door to what Pa Low felt was "the pattern of approach" to heathen Karen. Though he would live out his life in Thailand, he would never march in step with the evangelism of our border hills.

Looking back I see that, in agreeing to take on the responsibility of evangelistic outreach to the hills, Pa Low thought that with an annual campaign he would then have at least eleven and one-half months each year to give himself to pastor ing the local Maw Dta congregation. Because I saw the vast, unmapped, uncounted area to be evangelized as a full-time, year-round job, it never entered my mind to pass on to Pa Low any of the teaching and pastoring duties I carried. What shocking disappointment and frustration he met in those first weeks in Maw Dta. He must have felt I had misled him, inviting him to minister and then not turning the ministry over to him. Any hopes he might have carried surely died when Keddy came, for Keddy took the position that would be called senior (or preaching) pastor.

After almost three years in Maw Dta, Pa Low decided to cut and work a hill field. I was most pleased that he chose an area close to No Day Bow. Though this village was very far away from us, some of the Christian men working in that area witnessed of their faith and two families had become interested. Bob Peters had then visited and led them into faith and commitment.

Pa Low must have felt a leap of faith when he heard of this, and he purposed to work a field close to this new Christian community. He would pastor them, teach them, and I'm sure he hoped to form them into a community that would attract the unsaved. I believe Pa Low was a great help to them in many ways, but he did not see the sort of attractive community develop that he felt was essential to drawing the unchurched into the church. He was never to be satisfied with evangelism and church growth as he was to meet it in Thailand.

The tragedy of the man's life seems all the more real in that the very month he died, ten years after he had moved to Thailand, there began to be a response to the gospel among both his relatives and the village where he had once lived.

It would be wrong to leave the impression that Pa Low and his family were never a help or blessing to the Thailand Karen churches. I am sure that this deeply committed man was often a spiritual influence to individuals. I would judge that the picture of Pa Low and his family did much to change the pattern of life in many Christian homes.

For instance, heathen Karen seldom sat down to eat as

families. They came home from their fields, each one to eat as he or she was ready or hungry. I have known of occasions when two or three of a household prepared and ate a chicken with their rice. Others of that family coming home later, tired and hungry, found nothing but cold rice for them to warm up and eat alone. Pa Low and his wife and three sons sat down together to eat. New Karen Christians stopped what they were doing to listen as Gaw Ga No Moe (Pa Low's wife) called her sons home to eat. They took note of how this family waited for each other and shared with each other. And the picture of the family seated on the floor at their low, round table, heads bowed in prayer of thanks for the meal they were about to eat, changed forever the eating habits of a score of families.

In my opinion, the most important teaching and blessing Pa Low and his family gave to Maw Dta had to do with their family relationships. Actually only Gaw Ga No was a son of the household. One of the boys was a nephew whose father was dead and whose mother was remarried with a growing family. Her new husband did not want the son of her previous marriage. But it was the third boy whose story would deeply stir some of the Maw Dta family and influence the course of our church life.

Jaw A Cree had been taken from the grave by Gaw Ga No Moe. This boy's natural mother died in childbirth. Heathen custom in Burma among the hill Karen is the same as on our side of the border: the newborn baby will be buried with the mother, even if it is alive and healthy. Gaw Ga No Moe, happening on such a burial as she walked in the woods one day, reacted with Christian compassion and a fierce determination that defeated every argument of the gravediggers. In defiance of their fear and anger, she walked off with the baby.

Jaw A Cree was in his early teens by the time the family moved to Thailand, and he was a source of wonder to the Karen. I did not know his story in those days when the family lived with me and so could not understand why Karen after Karen would say of the boy, with a note of awe in their voice, "He's so valuable!" They were all remembering the haunting cry of a baby being buried alive with its dead mother. Every adult in our village had known of just such cases in their family circle in years gone by — a baby unwanted and buried alive.

Pa Low did not need to preach about the value of life. He did not need to say one word against the animist custom of burying a baby with its mother. The village watched Jaw A Cree hunt and fish and play and tease. We listened as he made up riddles and led the boys in pranks. And the village verdict was, "He's so valuable." The Lord taught through this family the truth that Satan, using the customs and rules of spirit worship, had robbed their families and villages of valuable sons and daughters — and that they did not ever again need to be so plundered.

Only eternity will reveal all the ways in which Pa Low brought blessing to the Karen church, but coming to the position of an evangelist he was a disappointment to me. I must balance that against the bitter disappointment I must have been to him. And it all started with a misunderstanding. We used the same words, but we meant something entirely different. By the time I understood what Pa Low meant by evangelism, it was too late to stop and go back and start over again.

Chapter 12

The Offense of the Message or The Offensiveness of the Messenger?

Keddy was with us for just nine months in Maw Dta. I felt that he had the most to contribute to the church family for he was an enormously gifted preacher and a born organizer and leader. He almost organized me off the face of the earth!

Keddy truly accomplished a great deal. But he was an idea man. Perhaps that's true of all leaders. He conceived plans that called for many workers. Life would often have been more relaxed if he had planned only for what he himself could perform, but instead his projects put others to work. Many of his projects first had to be put on paper and duplicated on our spirit duplicating machine. How often I have worked by the light of a smoky kerosene lamp to complete the duplicated pages he needed the next day for teaching or picturing a Bible story. Some of Keddy's projects were practical work projects: the youth of the church leveling an area where we would one day build a more permanent church, or cutting away the weeds from our playing field. For such an occasion he would give me the job of preparing and serving a meal to the workers.

Keddy assigned to me the teaching of the young people's Sunday School before the Sunday worship service that now started on the dot at 10:00 A.M. I was also to be responsible for a ladies meeting each week. Keddy was most disconcerted that men would come to a ladies meeting and adults to the young people's Sunday School class. Me, he could organize.

The Maw Dta congregation, he could not!

He had his way in starting the morning services on the dot of ten, but I feel it was too costly a victory, for many who loved the Lord hated being so regimented. These were a people who just did not live by the clock. There was a story often referred to by the church family. Mu Lay Bpa, traveling on a bus in the Maesod area, was wearing a watch which he had picked up for a friend at the watch repairman's. When another on the bus discovered his own watch had stopped, he asked Mu Lay Bpa for the correct time. Now Mu Lay Bpa had no idea how to read the face of the watch, but holding his arm up he squinted past it to the afternoon sun and judged the time to be 3:30. He must have been close as he boldly proclaimed that time, for two other men on the bus immediately corrected their watches by Mu Lay Bpa's pronouncement.

Keddy in no way sought to change or organize the trips I took to villages close around to talk to interested individuals or to encourage and teach those believing in the Lord. He really was not interested in that kind of outreach at all. I wish I had known how to evaluate that. But I did not. Keddy was concentrating his ministry on the choir.

Keddy's own ministry of preaching and teaching was always a blessing to me. He had a love for the Word of God and so carefully prepared his messages that they were always full of truth and very applicable.

He taught the young people to read music and formed them into a choir that eventually was very good. At first there were a few painful weeks when the tenors were always off key, the sopranos were too loud for the other voices, and if the basses had any complication of timing to their part they might as well have been singing a different piece altogether. But Keddy worked hard and soon had his choir hearing both time and harmony, and in the time he was with us he taught them to sing an amazing number of anthems.

I thought that the church appreciated his ministry and that even the unsaved were fond of him. I cannot express the shock it was, then, to receive a telegram while I was at our mission's annual conference meeting in Tak that told me Keddy had been murdered. Bay Law Bpa had run with the news to a Karen refugee from Burma living in Maesod and the refugee had sent the telegram.

In the early evening just as the kerosene lamps were lit, Keddy had sat down on the floor of Mu Lay Bpa's porch with a ring of young people about him. By the light of the lantern in the center he was teaching them some new song. The porch must have shown up as a lighted stage, and suddenly out at the edge of darkness where the jungle surrounded the village a gun was fired. The lamp exploded and Keddy's startled cry of pain sent echoes reverberating through our valley. His head was shattered by the homemade gunshot that had split up into a dozen or more ricocheting fragments. From all accounts I heard in the weeks that followed, Keddy suffered dreadfully before he died almost an hour later. Astoundingly, he died comforting those who were trying to help him as he assured them he was going into the presence of the Lord with his sins forgiven.

It was a time of horror for the Christians whose homes were close enough to know what had happened and had gathered to help. I have been amazed that there were so many children and young people in the group which tried to help save this young pastor's life. Even tiny children were allowed to watch the entire experience of Keddy's suffering and death. I cannot understand how they can be so unscarred by that night's experience.

Duane and Jackie Olson, who were in Thai work and had never even visited the Karen area of the WEC work, offered to drive me as far as the road went in the direction of Maw Dta and to walk with me the rest of the way into the village. Though civilization had so advanced that a road now came to within a few hours' walk of Maw Dta, this was still a real outworking of fellowship, for it not only meant that the Olsons must be away from a good bit of the conference when things would be discussed that would affect them and their work, but it also meant that they would be coming into a very tense situation with me. All we knew at that point was that a servant of the Lord had been put to death. Moreover, the Olsons were very conscious that for the few hours they were in Maw Dta they might do something that would offend Karen custom. But Duane and Jackie so entered into my confusion and sorrow and so compassionately greeted the Christians of the village that they left behind them a picture of what it is to weep with those who weep. This was not their sorrow, but they obviously had taken it up and would bear it with us.

The church family was in a state of confusion and near panic.

"We are all going to be killed," a neighbor announced in despair.

"We must scatter to the hills," headman Pa Gu Der, grandson-in-law of Maw Dta, judged.

"We must move to Burma," Mu Lay Bpa decided.

"Don't go anywhere alone and don't light your lamp at night," headman Cad Way advised me.

I would like for you to think that I was so calm, cool and collected that I was not at all moved by Cad Way's warning. The truth is that it so upset me that every nighttime sound set my heart racing. Chickens settling for the night, the squeal of a pig ousted from its mother's side, even the eerie sound of bamboo moved by the wind to creak and cry as it bends and scrapes its giant branches was enough to reduce me to a shivering idiot without a sensible thought in my head. When fire was lit beneath a clump of bamboo, causing each joint to explode with a bang, it sounded as if the village was being invaded by a band of robbers, each firing a repeater rifle. All I could hope was that they would get it over with quickly. Whoever they were, just let them shoot straight enough that I might die without too much suffering. Some thoughtful soul had suggested that perhaps I would be shot through the open wooden slats of my porch flooring, so I discovered I was developing cramps in my legs as I tried to walk without putting my feet down! Somehow the idea of a bullet through the bottom of my foot was just too much! And of course, all this time I was trying to comfort and reassure the church family.

"Why, Lord?" I kept asking. But I did not ask for long. Eventually I began to listen. I believe that the Lord who is not silent was always answering that question, if only I had stopped my crying of "why?" long enough to listen. I began to understand some things that I suppose ought to be rather evident to any inquiring Christian. Though many times my lips have asked, "Why, Lord?" my heart has meant, "How could you allow . . . ?" Of course, that is unconscious blasphemy and will never be answered.

Why? There are obviously three levels of answer to that question in the affairs of life. There are the motives of man, the plans of Satan, and the eternal purposes of God.

I began to understand that many men in our area had been offended by Keddy. Along with Pa Low and Johnson, Keddy had the same idea of evangelism: an attractive community drawing in the unchurched. So Keddy set to work to mold us into an attractive community according to his taste. To his way of thinking, in order for us to become attractive our speech had to change. Our hillbilly talk offended his ear and he wanted us to speak like the highly educated Karen of Rangoon. He ridiculed the speech of our area, and on the young people of his choir he went to work to stamp out what he felt were mistakes in pronunciation and expression. So successfully did he change their speech that there soon came a day when parents could hardly understand what their children were saying. More than one father completely lost his temper when corrected by his teenage daughter. And I surely understood, for I too had lost my temper over this sort of thing and could readily sympathize with the fathers.

Once I had taken the four girls living with me to a meeting in Dry Creek, two hours' walk away. There were several girls in the meeting who were the same age as my girls. These Dry Creek girls were not Christians but they listened carefully to the lessons and had a lot of questions when the meeting was over. I thought this was a great opportunity for the Christian girls to share their faith with these ones of the same age and background. But the conversation had barely gotten started when the Maw Dta girls started to mimic and ridicule an expression the Dry Creek girls had used. I could almost hear the voice of their choir leader in their supercilious criticism of the language of the hill Karen. The disgusting thing was that the expression they were ridiculing was one they had habitually used themselves until just a few weeks before. Instead of this making the Christian community attractive to the unsaved it caused hurt and embarrassment. As a result, we lost all opportunity to have any impact on the girls of Dry Creek.

After Keddy's death I realized that even the Christian adults were deeply offended at this relentless struggle to change their way of speech. I could see the endeavor as something that would be a hindrance to the spread of the gospel. To change pronunciation, sentence structure and idioms made it almost impossible for the unsaved to understand what the Christians were talking about.

Keddy, Johnson and Pa Low all put much emphasis on manners, health and cleanliness to perfect the attractive community. But it was Keddy who caused the most offense because of his manner. He was the best educated of the three, with both college and seminary behind him, yet that would not have mattered if he had had the wisdom to act humbly before the older men and women of the village. But Keddy's manner was arrogant, and the criticisms he made to his choir children about our village speech and customs did not lose in the telling. If anything, they became more deadly with every telling. I am convinced that it was the arrogant picture he presented and not his message that brought offense. The tragedy is that the arrogance was a pose Keddy thought would impress the illiterate, inexperienced Karen of Thailand. He assumed they would not appreciate his education; it was muscle and brash confidence, not brains, these simple people admired, he thought. So he acted tough. He was too immature, and so was I, to realize that the people were impressed all right — they were inflamed to hatred.

On the surface the murderers were motivated by hatred for

this young man of their own age who seemed to think so highly of himself and to so despise them. Though the three young men who eventually were revealed to be the ones responsible for the killing were opposed also to the gospel, their conversation revealed that it was personal hatred that motivated them. For them it was not a cause, it was a person. And they felt sure an offended village would approve their action.

Of course there was deeper motivation, for Satan and evil forces are real. This was an area where everyone had bowed to their authority for centuries. Keddy was an organizer and a spokesman, and I have never doubted that the ancient plan to kill the shepherd so that the sheep would be scattered was repeated in Maw Dta. It almost succeeded. For many months after Keddy's death there was still talk among Christians about moving away from the village. I did not feel that I could advise anyone. Perhaps this scattering of His people would be a part of God's plan for us. Over the centuries He has allowed persecution to scatter His own again and again. If everyone did move away and scatter in the hills, perhaps somewhere out where the gospel had not yet gone we would eventually have a repeat Antioch. But the talk of moving died down as the church family realized that the murderous rage was not aimed at us.

If on the human level the provocation was offense and if on the satanic level there was an effort to stop the growth of the church, God remained sovereign. Men and demons cannot frustrate His eternal plans. What did He purpose when He allowed a puny trio to execute His servant?

Just before I went to that annual mission conference when Keddy was killed, I received a letter from a missionary of another mission who had known Keddy just before he came to Maw Dta. This man, with real Christian concern for the Lord's work, felt he must tell of the circumstances that caused Keddy to flee to Maw Dta. He reported that Keddy had been in charge of a mission school and one of the students had been found to be pregnant. When questioned, the girl named Keddy as the father.

At the first reading I was dumbfounded. I could not believe it. Keddy had been with us for nine months and he had been most careful where girls were concerned. He never singled out anyone for special attention. He carefully observed the rules that forbade private conversation or even walking out of the village with just one girl. For the first seven months that he worked with the young people he had treated all the boys and girls alike.

It then came as a complete surprise when Keddy told me one day that he felt Dee Paw, Mu Lay Bpa's eldest living daughter, was the one God had chosen to be his life partner. If that was a surprise, you can imagine what a shock it was when his next pronouncement was that, because he had no parents living in the area, he wanted me to act in the stead of his mother . . . and not only tell Dee Paw's parents of his desire to marry their daughter but to propose to the girl for him!

Two years earlier I had played a somewhat different part. Jaw Lu, a grandson of Maw Dta, made his choice of a wife. His mother, however, was violently opposed to the union. Jaw Lu had made up his mind to go ahead with it against her wishes, but he had no proper channels to move through and so he wrote a letter. The problem was that the girl could not read, so she brought the letter to Massey and me to read to her. When the shock of the message had worn off, Ee Naw turned to me shyly and said, "You can write the reply." I got settled with pencil and paper and looked at her — expecting her to tell me what to write. With much giggling and hiding behind her hands she finally got it across to me that I was to word the reply myself. That was hard enough, but I didn't even know if she wanted the answer to be yes or no! A half hour of perspiration and frustration passed before I found that she *did* want to marry him. I don't know what I said in that letter, but since they are a happily married couple with six children and even Jaw Lu's mother seems pleased about it, I must have said the right thing.

At the time Keddy talked to me of his desire to marry Dee Paw, I could not see anything to hinder this except that I felt like a silly fool proposing for him. However, Keddy was quite adamant that this was the proper way to do it. No dates had been set, but Dee Paw's family was happy about the coming marriage and Dee Paw seemed to return Keddy's love.

I wondered, then, when I read the story of sin and shame in Keddy's past life, could it be true? Could this be why he had come alone, with no friends to escort and help carry his things as had been the case with Pa Low and Johnson? Was this story of weakness and fall in his past the reason why he was so careful of the girls in Maw Dta and why he insisted on my entering into the proposal and wedding arrangements?

I knew I would have to talk to him about the letter I had received and I felt sure that this was going to be one of the most difficult conversations of my life. I hoped that during the field conference I would get some idea of how to go about that confrontation. But, of course, during conference word came that Keddy had been murdered.

Though there was absolutely nothing in Keddy's life during that nine months he lived in Maw Dta that would cause one to suspect such weakness and sin in his past, I have always felt certain in my heart that the story was true — and especially from the moment I heard of Keddy's death. I believe that the Lord gave His child a chance for a short ministry to prove that he could walk above the temptation that had once ruined his testimony and ministry. Keddy proved the Lord's help in those short months of ministry in Thailand and then the Lord took him home. No man as gifted as Keddy could have gone on seeing and teaching the holiness of God and the righteous position and practice of the Lord's children while covering up such sin in his own past. He surely held up the purity of Christ in his teaching, and I began to wonder then if Keddy did not see that purity with a heavy and convicted heart.

As the letter had reported it, the girl claimed Keddy to be responsible for her condition and then, before any judgment could be made, Keddy disappeared. It was months before anyone knew where he had gone. When they found out, this one whom I believe to have been a true friend to Keddy wrote me all of the story he knew.

When I heard that Keddy had been killed, I was much upset; but at the same time there was an underlying thankfulness that it was not the Lord's plan for Keddy to be faced with his sin in Maw Dta, where forgiveness would have been incomplete. The church would doubtless have asked him to step down from pastoral ministry and I very much doubt that Dee Paw would have wanted to marry him. The fact that the girl involved in the sin was just a schoolgirl in her mid-teens put such a burden of blame on Keddy that I could not picture the men of Maw Dta accepting him as a part of the family community at all.

I do not feel that God acted in law, to cut off a sinner from the earth, but rather that He acted in grace to spare a repentant son from the shame and recriminations that would follow the making public of his sin in a small community. If Keddy's sin could have cut off God's grace, then it would not have been grace.

I was comforted, then, with what I believe God showed me of the reasons behind the killing of Keddy. On the human level, offense and hate; on the satanic level, spiritual conflict aiming to stop the church, to slay the shepherd and scatter the sheep; but in the eternal councils of a sovereign God, a decision to deal with a son in grace and love.

Chapter 13

Another Nancy!

In my mind Pa Low was responsible for the evangelistic out-reach to the hills and Keddy was taking hold as pastor of the Maw Dta congregation . . . when Johnson, the third worker from Burma, joined us. Time would show that neither Keddy nor Pa Low fitted the job given him. Keddy, with every spiritual gift that qualified him to teach and minister the Word, was far too abrasive in his personality to truly pastor a group that needed to be fed and encouraged. Pa Low could not really consider the hundreds of villages needing to be reached right now. His mind was set for the Christian family to go displaying the attractiveness of community in order to influence one target village each year. Our generation, dying right now in the hills of Thailand, would never have the opportunity to hear the gospel with this kind of evangelism.

As ill-placed as were Pa Low and Keddy, yet it was Johnson who was perhaps the most out of place of the three who came from Burma. Both Keddy and Johnson had Western names; exposure to the English language and literature led them to choose names that suited their fancy. That was fine for me. But the Karen could not even *pronounce* Johnson's name!

When Johnson came to Maw Dta, about one third of the Sunday morning congregation was from headman Cad Way's village, a twenty-minute walk away from us across a rice field. Only a few of this group could return for the evening service or Wednesday night prayer meeting. And I couldn't blame them.

Our evening meetings were always early because we had no electricity, but on a cloudy evening in the rainy season even by 6:30 that field could be a murky obstacle course. Stumps, rocks, tangled vines and deep mud holes would be completely hidden in the mist or rain. The Karen would hardly consider as difficult the two streams that had to be crossed, one on each side of the field. But to me, the two and sometimes three feet of water — and at flood season four feet — to be waded through were the last straw! To be honest, I was amazed that so many came regularly on Sunday mornings!

In considering how Johnson could best serve the church in Thailand, I began to think of Cad Way's village. If Johnson held services for them in their own village, would that convenience be a blessing or would it be harmful? I knew that most of those who crossed the field to worship on Sunday mornings would often stay for hours visiting friends and relatives in our village. Most of them would stop for a time at my house on leaving the church. Listening to their conversations on my porch, I came to feel that the informal Christian visiting was of great value and blessing. But balanced in my mind was a picture of the blessing and the testimony of gathering in their own village. I realized that only one or two of the youth in Cad Way's village were a part of the choir, for evening practice sessions were out of the question for most of them, and none attended Sunday evening worship.

Because Cad Way's village seemed to me to be missing out on so much that the community of Maw Dta enjoyed, I decided to ask Johnson to pastor the Christians of Cad Way. And I thought I was giving them the best of the three from Burma. For Johnson was a different personality from Keddy. Though they were both about twenty-seven years old, from the same sort of background and with much the same sort of training, they were very different in their outward reactions to the people of Maw Dta. Johnson had a rather sweet manner and there was never a bit of arrogance in his way with the hill Karen. He never appeared proud or critical, and the saved and unsaved of Maw Dta seemed to love him.

I have seen Johnson cook a chicken for a widow who had been ill for days and found that nothing tasted good. I have seen him sit visiting with the elderly who hardly gave him a chance to get a word in, and I knew that he was listening to stories of men and women long gone from this earth and only remembered by those who sat out their last days dreaming in the sun and longing for just such an ear as Johnson's to listen and listen and listen. And Johnson was terribly interested, maybe not in the people spoken of, but in the people talking.

I was thrilled with Johnson's deep commitment and his obvious love for the Lord. I felt certain this one would be a blessing and encouragement to Cad Way's village, and I felt that village just across the fields from us was a choice harvest field. I had no doubt in my mind that I was handing Johnson a harvest to be envied around the world. I was wrong on all counts!

But God, rich in mercy, did not let me see the confusion and crash of my visions until I had a co-worker who would stand with me in fellowship and encouragement.

Before any of the three had come from Burma I heard that a new WEC missionary, Nancy Guy, felt called of God to work with the Karen. (That's right, *another* Nancy.) Just before I was to meet this Scottish nurse who was already studying the Thai language, Ellen Gillman, who had already met Nancy, was telling me about her. "She is such a great nurse; she would rather nurse you than talk to you," Ellen proclaimed.

Ellen is almost always very careful and conservative in her speech, so the few times that she breaks out into outrageousness I always find to be really funny. Once I heard her remonstrating with Joeky as they were facing a very complicated problem in the church they were working with. "We'll cross that bridge when we burn it behind us," she announced with a straight face. I realize that when she gets that outrageous, Ellen surprises and amuses herself. And I'm sure that was true of the statement she made about my future co-worker who would "rather nurse you than talk to you."

I could not help but laugh at the ridiculous picture this

painted, but at the same time it caused me to think and to wonder about the adjustments of a real nurse to the dirty, sickly Karen. If Nancy tried to make them change, they would be offended. Would Nancy be able to appreciate that the Christians had already made tremendous changes; and could the Karen realize that every new change Nancy would ask would mean life and health?

Even the Christians had little respect for foreign medicine, and no idea at all of taking medicine under directions. In those days when Maw Dta was first introduced to foreign medicine, to tell someone they should take two pills three times a day was to absolutely insure that they would not take two pills three times a day! That you put them under orders was enough to insure that any self-respecting Karen would automatically break out of that subordinate position and do something different. I felt that I had to become a devious sneak, manipulating conversations until the Karen thought they had decided quite on their own to take medicine just as it was prescribed on the bottle. When I knew my patients well I was quite capable of advising them to take just half the strength of medicine I wanted them to take, for I was certain that when they got home they would begin to figure that if one pill is good, two pills are twice as good. I don't suppose that is good nursing ethics, but it happens to be good Karen psychology. I did not doubt that a good nurse would be appalled.

There was another dimension to this dispensing of medicine in Maw Dta: I never charged for anything. Every pill that was given out was given without a price tag or strings attached. I heard continually from other missionaries in Thailand and around the world that people do not appreciate what they do not pay for; therefore, do not give, sell! I never seriously considered this course. Long before the Karen were free to use our foreign medicine I realized that most Karen who needed medicine had no cash. If I charged, perhaps a tenth of those who needed medicine would be able to pay on the spot. Should I keep accounts and count as debtors those who did not pay? If I charged some and gave to others, those who paid would not be offended — the Karen are a proud people, and those who could pay would be proud of their payments. But those who could not pay would be shamed and would not again accept charity. Medicine would become a status symbol of the wealthy few. If I wanted the poor to receive freely, then those with money would have to receive freely as well.

Selling or giving away medicine were not the only options, as there was another way; but it was too long and too hard a way, and I was not willing to do the bookkeeping. Almost everyone who received medicine eventually gave me some sort of return gift. If I was going to think in terms of trade instead of gifts then I was going to have some strange bookkeeping to do. How much are three huge bullfrogs (still alive) worth in terms of aspirin and quinine? How much are three duck eggs (one rotten) worth in terms of sulfaguanidine? This bookkeeping was just beyond me. If people could not appreciate what they could not pay for then they would just have to get cured without appreciating it!

But since I could diagnose few illnesses I only spent about twenty dollars a month on medicine in those early days. A nurse would want more and different kinds of medicine to treat the ill. If she felt she wanted to continue as I had started, giving freely, the growing expense might cause her real problems. But the most likely situation was that she would so disapprove of giving free medicine that she would feel she must charge a fee. And I would need to defend her action to a resentful Karen people.

I dreaded meeting Nancy and explaining that I'd been giving, not selling, medicine.

I had been around enough nurses on the mission field to realize that Joeky and Mary were truly exceptions. Joeky never spoke of her nursing experiences and Mary only mentioned the funny things, or on occasion would meet me at the breakfast table with the glum announcement that she had had a dreadful nightmare: she had dreamed she was back on night duty! But most nurses revel in the talk of hospitals and cases and the comparing of medicines and nursing experiences. The most gory details seemed to be brought out at meal time! Since nursing had been one of Nancy's life interests, I could not afford to be disinterested. But I doubted if I would be able to work up any real enthusiasm for the subject and I felt that my lack of stimulating interest would amputate Nancy from one of the loves of her life, for I was going to be the only person she could talk to for a great deal of time, until she became fluent in the Karen language. After a year of Thai study she would begin Karen study in Maesod, but she would move to Maw Dta long before Karen conversation became easy for her.

That Nancy was a nurse had been so stressed that that was the thing that concerned me first. But being thorough about it, I quickly moved on to problem number two: she was from Scotland. Would she feel that everything Scottish was best and right? Oh dear, would I have to start eating oatmeal without sugar for breakfast every day?

I had realized that while I loved Mary from England, Joeky from Holland and Ellen from Canada, adjustments for us had been super-colossal exercises. Nothing came easily or naturally in the relationships with these co-workers from different backgrounds. Variety might be the spice of life, but life just gets too spicy when you have adjusted to two foreign cultures (Thai and Karen) and a parade of co-workers from different countries. With the stream of constant change, differences began to annoy . . . and my lifestyle had become a crazy quilt of compromise and adjustments. And with my recent adjustment to workers from Burma, I just did not feel very pliable anymore.

The first day I met Nancy Guy in Tak, she and I spent the evening exchanging jokes with Mark Overgaard, who was home on vacation from high school in Malaysia. It was such a relief to realize that, like myself, Nancy's sense of humor had stopped developing at about the level of a sixteen-year-old. I knew that laughter would help cushion some of the trials and problems of isolated living in primitive conditions. Nancy would need to be able to laugh, and I could feel myself relaxing that evening as again and again Nancy's laughter bubbled over at the ridiculous, irrational and incredible jokes Mark told.

One incident stands out over the years to let me know that I found Nancy Guy unbelievably easy to be with. She was on her very first visit to Maw Dta and was in the village over a weekend. One of the things that was always a concern was what to feed guests. There was no market and not everyone wants to eat strange leaves, roots and ferns from the rain forest. If Nancy did move into Maw Dta she would inevitably learn to like some of these things, but there was no way to more surely guarantee that a guest will get an upset stomach than to feed her several meals of unadulterated Maw Dta food.

When my mailman took my outgoing mail every two weeks or so he would bring back (along with my mail) a few groceries from the missionaries in Maesod. But a head of cabbage, a dozen eggs, a few string beans and a kilo of pork, fried and salted, would arrive after the twenty-mile trip a bit squashed and wilted. Every once in a while there would be a food parcel from family or friends in America. I always saved some of the foodstuffs from these parcels to feed guests, and though there was never enough to feed guests foreign (that is, Western) meals throughout a very long stay, I could at least plan that there were some things they could eat and enjoy every day of their stay. But the Sunday of Nancy's visit had been particularly hectic. There had been Karen guests all day long. We had had a meal at noon after the morning church service and, as every Sunday, that meal had been pure Karen so that guests from the hills would feel comfortable eating with us. We sat on the floor around a low round table eating rice with our fingers. The spicy dishes eaten with rice were assuredly delicious to the Karen asbestos palate, but appallingly hot to a Westerner. Poor Nancy had just pushed some of the stuff around on her plate and must have really been hungry long before time for the evening meal. Some guests had stayed right through the evening service, so we had had no opportunity for a meal before the church gong had sounded, summoning us to worship.

As I have explained, the evening service was always quite early since we had no electricity. The meeting was over at 6:00

or 6:30, just as it was getting dark. It was quite often my practice to wait until after that service to have my evening meal, although there was no set pattern. That night there were relays of guests visiting until well after 8:00. I was dead tired after the last guests finally left. Exhausted, I suggested that we have an evening drink of tea or coffee and go to bed. Nancy, looking not the least bit dismayed, asked if it would be all right if she had a slice of bread with her drink. And then it hit me! I had completely forgotten to serve my guest an evening meal. The most graphic proof that Nancy had been easy to have around was that I had forgotten to feed her. What could be easier than a guest you don't have to feed?

With a very red face I got the previously prepared meal out of the refrigerator (a kerosene refrigerator given to me by a Bible class in California while I was on my first furlough). I do not remember what that meal consisted of, but it was a very important meal for it proved to me that I was not going to get ulcers worrying about how to please a Scottish palate! Nancy certainly was not going to demand that I make drastic changes in my lifestyle. She was willing to go to bed hungry if that's what it cost to fit into life in Maw Dta. She would be lucky if I remembered to feed her at all!

Before Nancy made her first visit to Maw Dta I gave her a nickname that, to my joy, so caught the Karen mind that it stuck — and she was never given another nickname. Karen always nicknamed any guest or foreigner they met. I was "Auntie Tall." Ellen was "Auntie Freckle." But there were others who would have been very insulted if they had understood their nicknames. The Karen did not think they were being insulting; they just picked out what to them was an obvious feature and used that for the nickname. Nancy had a weight problem and maintained that just to look at food made her gain weight. Most of the Karen have tiny bones and are quite thin. I was apprehensive of the name they might give her, so I told the children that they could call her "Auntie Tickle." With little children climbing all over us they soon found if we had a ticklish spot. I knew Nancy really was ticklish and warned them not to torment her. "Auntie Tickle" sounds cute in Karen — Goo Gwee — and the Karen liked it; so did Nancy. She would appreciate her nickname even more when later she could understand Karen and heard the villagers calling another of the missionaries "Auntie Steep Seat" and another "Auntie Bug Eyes."

Auntie Tall and Auntie Tickle were going to have to make many adjustments to live and work together. It would not be automatic. I'm sure Nancy did have many misgivings about dispensing medicine without cost, but she kept to herself any criticisms she had. By the time she had lived in the village a few months she was as persuaded as I that that was the only way we could be of medical help to these people cut off from all but the medicines of spirit worship. If there were other areas where Nancy initially questioned my judgment, she waited to express her criticisms until she was at home with the Karen culture, and by that time most criticisms were gone. Where there was still disagreement about policy or practice, Nancy's ideas never came across as negative faultfinding but as positive, constructive help. There were rough places, but I found, as that evening spent with Mark Overgaard had promised, Nancy could cushion the hard places with her sense of humor.

I remember one afternoon when hill guests had departed and we almost laughed ourselves silly. A very elderly lady had been brought to us by Christian friends. She was suffering from a "deadly" complaint. The wind was escaping out of her ears, saying "Boop! boop! boop!" That sounded bad to me. I was tempted to think we should quickly put cotton in her ears before she went flat like a tire. But Nancy felt that this might be a symptom of anemia. She shone her flashlight (in Scotland, that's a torch) into the woman's eyes and gave her instructions on how to take the iron pills she was counting out. Nancy thought her instructions were complete until, with fascination, she watched the woman insert her first dose — one pill in each ear! You can see how strange our medicine was to hill Karen. Her complaint involved her ears; Nancy looked into her eyes and gave her medicine to put in her mouth.

As the weeks passed and I got to know Nancy Guy better and better, I had to marvel. The Lord had chosen us to work together, yet at first consideration it seemed most unlikely that we'd fit together. The normal adjustment one has to make to a co-worker from nine to five — after which you then part company, to go home to your own inclinations and interests — is one thing. But to mesh one's lifestyle with a companion who is right there at every conversation is clearly another matter. But God had made the right choice — Nancy would make the adjustments. She would fit into Maw Dta and I would be absolutely delighted with her as a companion.

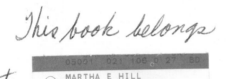

(1) *Nancy Guy and a friend.*
(2) *Wa Paw: her parents thought she was retarded.*
(3) *A Karen kitchen.*

Chapter 14

Body Life Across Culture Barriers

I needed to remind myself that during my first visit to the village of Maw Dta it had impressed me as nothing more than a few moldy bamboo huts, straggling without plan down the hilly slope to the river whose banks were slippery with the muddy tracks of pigs, water buffalo and elephants. I needed to remember that there had been nothing in the village to make me want to live there. It was my response to God moving in my heart that brought me to Maw Dta, and not my response to the village.

I needed to remember this when I saw Nancy Guy battling with adjustments, struggling to accept the primitive living conditions; for the years had worked a great change in my feelings toward the Karen and their hills. What I once despised, I now loved. With shame I must admit it was not just the village but the people of the village that I at first rejected. So I needed to now give Nancy time to see past the dirty bodies with their marks of disease and illness. Even though the Christians now bathed every day, it did not take long, walking barefoot through forests or working under the grueling sun in a rice field, to acquire a layer of dust — and clothing washed in a sandy stream is never sparkling clean! With time Nancy would see past this dirt to the beauty of this graceful people. She would soon see the perfection of their white teeth and the beauty of their black eyes. Their dark coloring was so restful against the brilliance of their tropical forests in rainy season and the blinding baked-copper of their fields in dry season. Their quietness was so peaceful when all the air of their mountain world was full of sounds: water rushing, wind shrieking, and thousands of insects, birds and forest animals calling, crying, piping, drumming, ringing, singing. But eyes new to the Karen world saw surface dirt, grimy clothing, the scars and marks of illness and disease. Every home was decorated with the marks of poverty.

Nancy faced this constant barrage of sight and sound that demanded her acceptance. As I watched her change and adapt, I realized with new insight that there were certain problems in the Karen church to which neither Nancy nor I could adjust. There were situations where we had to demand *change*, not of ourselves, but of the church. We had to see change in the Karen if the church was to survive as a people on earth rightly related to God in heaven.

I watched Nancy accepting the Karen and demanding change of herself to align herself with them, and I rejoiced. I also saw her stiffen to an unyielding position when suddenly it was no longer human culture but God's standard of holiness that was at issue. I then realized afresh that though personal adjustment is difficult for us humans, it is sometimes even harder to stand unyielding and demand that others change. But as servants of the Lord, that stand is not optional. We cannot compromise His holiness.

When it came to our church problems that followed Keddy's murder, because of our foreignness it was not always possible for us to see just where that unyielding stand should be taken. We watched the unfolding drama with a desperate plea that the Lord would clearly show us what we had to accept as Karen — people loved by Him just the way they were — and what was Karen that had to be transformed into the image of Christ.

Shortly after the murder of Keddy it began to be circulated quite openly that it was three young men who had gone together in the dusk to murder the pastor. Two of these suspects were married and in no way related to any of the Christians. But the third, a single fellow — who, rumor said, was the one who fired the gun — was the son of Day Zay and a grandson of Maw Dta.

At least twenty adult Christians were closely related to the suspected killer, and that carved the church into two hurting sections: those related to Jaw Naw Ay felt guilty and defensive; those who were not related to him were judging with deep resentment. But it was not so much Jaw Naw Ay they were judging with their quiet eyes; according to their tribal law and the law of God he was a killer and without excuse. Rather, they were quietly waiting for his loved ones in the church family to act. Would they excuse an inexcusable crime?

Keddy had no family in Maw Dta to demand justice — no mother or father, sisters or brothers to be clamoring now for his death to be avenged. No, that is not true — for as abrasive as Keddy was in personality, still, on the spiritual level he was brother, son, and loved one in the church family. His death caused even those of the Christian community who were most offended by him to now realize that he was a part of them and his death was their loss. The very silence and quiet waiting of the Christians was a thundering voice demanding justice, and it was the Christians related to Jaw Naw Ay who were truly on trial now.

It all seemed so strange and foreign to me, and what a comfort it was that I was not alone but had Nancy's companionship. We could not understand why tribal justice could not have dealt with this. But we were learning that there are only two kinds of punishment in Karen customs. An offender is fined for lesser crimes and pays the fine to the offended family. But if a crime is an offense against society, exposing villagers to danger and corruption, the offender is executed. There is nothing between those two alternatives, for there was no way of imprisoning or rehabilitating an offender.

Only once had I known of a Karen being physically restrained, and that was not because he was a criminal but because he was insane and presented danger to himself and others. Thinking back to that man and his condition, I could see why small Karen villages could not undertake to restrain and punish.

It was close to the end of my first term when that incident occurred. Mary was away helping nurse a sick missionary on another station; Massey was also away one afternoon during Mary's absence, so I was alone. I had a touch of malaria, so, dosed with quinine, I went to bed. Every room of our house opened out onto an open porch, and we had hasps and locks on our doors to lock the outside of each door when we went away; but it had never seemed necessary to be able to lock any room when we were at home. Karen just did not lock their houses when they were at home. In fact, the common way of locking a house when the family was away was just to take down the bamboo ladder leading up to the porch. Of course, anyone who was really set on robbing just had to prop the ladder back in place. But, as Karen will remind you, anyone who is really set on robbing can easily remove a bamboo wall or piece of bamboo flooring. The Karen felt the only way to really stop robberies was to execute the robbers. For thousands of years Karen found that to be the effective way to deal with the problem and left locks to the rest of the world. One day this would change, with the coming of roads.

Never had I felt that my unlocked door exposed me to danger, but that afternoon, in feverish apprehension, I felt I had to secure that door somehow. The door opened inward, so the simplest thing to do was just to move the foot of my bed to obstruct the opening of the door. I awoke from a feverish sleep to find that a man of the village who had been acting strangely for some time had opened the door to its limit of two or three inches and had reached in and grabbed my foot. With one eye pressed to the opening, he was jabbering away with curses and obscenities. I could hardly hear my own voice as I called for help, but it was loud enough to reach a child playing outside. Within moments, there was a group of men there to lead away my tormentor. As the sound of his shouting and struggling echoed up through the village I could only stare at the foot of my bed, feeling weak with thankfulness to the Lord that He had moved me to a precaution that had never before been necessary. The man was most certainly insane. Led away, he was first chained to one of his house posts with huge elephant chains. Only the strongest men of the village dared go close to him, for he quickly learned to use that chain that bound him as a dangerous weapon. The area within reach of the chain was soon cleared of every removable thing, as he pelted anyone who approached him with stones, rocks, roots and twigs. Within a few days he was moved, to be secured to a clump of bamboo outside the village, for he had begun to tear down his house and the bamboo beams became dangerous missiles in his hands.

His screams and vile threats echoed through the village day and night. Calling us by name, he screamed abuse and such fearful threats that every villager was in terror that the chain that bound him might at any moment snap, setting him free. As a village, we began to feel we were all as imprisoned in the tragedy as was the insane one. But never would village elders put to death a man with a mental illness. That was never an option in their thinking. If one was ill, all would suffer with him, and at his death he was mourned as the man he once was and not as the stranger he became, ranting outside the village, bound with elephant chains.

The village was not a prison, and no way could corrective punishment be imposed on Jaw Naw Ay by the men of Maw Dta. Though Karen had never turned one of their own over to Thai justice, I could not help but feel, as Thai officials came to investigate Keddy's death, that surely this was the right thing to do. As an outsider, I could not even begin to understand how drastic a course I was expecting.

Jaw Naw Ay, stupified by drugs, could only claim that he hated Keddy. But now that the personality that had so irritated him was gone, he could hardly remember why he had so deep a malice against the preacher. I felt that I, too, waited in a wary silence. What could be done that would punish a killer and yet bring redemption to his crippled mind, and healing to our wounded community?

There were two others quietly watching, waiting and judging throughout those long months: Johnson and Pa Low. Whatever had been their hidden feeling about being foreigners on our side of the border now surfaced. Nancy and I could hardly bear to see Johnson appear on our porch, for his mind and talk dwelt always on the unavenged murder. Over and over again, the bitter question would come: "Will my murder, too, go unpunished?" Because of that distrust and bitterness there was no way Johnson could minister to the church or to the unsaved hills. I grew to long that he might return to Burma, yet I knew that that bitter, judgmental spirit needed to be healed first or it could sour all of his life and ministry.

Johnson came again and again to Nancy and me, sometimes visiting three times in one day. Yet his ears seemed completely stopped to anything we could say. He could not listen to us, and yet he kept coming. Nothing showed more plainly than those endless trips up our steps how alienated he had become in his mind from the life of Maw Dta.

Pa Low did not come to us nor do I believe he climbed the stairs to any other Christian home of our village in those months. We made a point of calling often on him and his family. At every visit we were received with politeness, yet conversation gave no real clue as to what Pa Low was thinking or feeling. By his silence, Pa Low was eloquently demanding justice.

As the months went by, Mu Lay Bpa was called again and again to appear before the police in Maeramard or Maesod. That Mu Lay Bpa had not been in the village when Keddy was shot seemed to be a meaningful lead to the Thai police, for they reasoned that if someone hired a killer to do away with his enemies, he would do so when he had a sure alibi. The police strongly suspected that Mu Lay Bpa had hired a killer to remove his daughter's fiance.

Mu Lay Bpa's family was under great strain, and all the time the village *knew* who had committed the murder. Pa Gu Der, the village headman, made no move to judge or punish. Was this because he was a brother-in-law of the murderer?

Even Mu Lay Bpa's family made no accusations while they themselves were suspected and questioned by the Thai authorities. But the mother of the murderer was sister to Mu Lay Moe. If the Mu Lay Bpa household exposed Jaw Naw Ay to the Thai authorities or demanded that tribal elders act in judgment, would a closely knit family be divided beyond repair? Though it was a most involved and complicated situation, right and wrong were not obscure; but the village and Christian community were silent.

All three of the young men who had gone together to commit the murder were opium addicts, but Jaw Naw Ay was unique in that he was also a drunkard. I lived in his village for years and only had one or two conversations with him. This was because he always seemed to be under the influence of drink or drugs, and any remark that I made would be met with a blank stare.

One day during those long months of waiting to see if justice would be done, as I was teaching a children's class in Cad Way's village I looked up to see Jaw Naw Ay silently watching me from the back of the group of children. I could tell nothing of his reaction to what I was saying for his face was a blank, almost as if he did not hear me at all. When the lesson was finished and we closed the class in prayer, I opened my eyes to find that he had gone as silently as he had joined the class.

Coming home from Cad Way and crossing a strip of heavy forest, a shallow river, a wide field, and then a second river, I kept scanning the low hills for the movement that would reveal a hidden sniper. I surely did not find it comfortable to live in a village where we knew there was a murderer loose. Yet I knew I felt only a tiny bit of tension compared to the tremendous tightening strain that pulled constantly at Mu Lay Bpa's family and on Johnson and Pa Low those months.

April was dragging to a blistering close. The temperature was up over 105 degrees day after day. The hills surrounding us were charred and black, for they had been cleared of trees and brush and set ablaze to be ready for planting as soon as the rains would come. The wind, then, from off those blackened hills was as a blast from an open furnace long before noon each day.

Coming home from Cad Way's village I was completely exposed if the killer watched, and I thought to myself how exposed we were then as a church family. Every weakness and failure lay open to view and we were vulnerable to blistering judgment.

If the rains did not come, our burned-off hills would be forever sterile; there would never again be a rice harvest in Maw Dta if God did not send His showers to our blackened hills. That was surely true, too, of our church family. We too were burned, not just by what had happened to Keddy but by our varied reactions to his murder. The breakdown of trust and fellowship had left us as barren as our hills.

Johnson continued to cross the fields to Cad Way's village for just a few weeks after Keddy's murder. He complained that the meetings were poorly attended, and only one or two of the young people had any interest in the Word preached. Finally I began to realize how desperate the situation had become. It was true: not even one-third of the Christians who had come faithfully across from the headman's village to worship in Maw Dta were attending the services Johnson held for them in their own village. In a conversation with Cad Way and several other leaders of the Christian community across the fields, I asked what they preferred. Did they want Johnson to continue to hold services in their village, or would they rather return to the larger meeting in Maw Dta?

I began to realize that Johnson, once so well liked, had somehow missed out with those from Cad Way's village. The quickly growing group had not just stopped growing, it was shrinking. Had Johnson suspected the men of Cad Way of having a part in the killing of Keddy? Had he appeared suspicious and judgmental in those days before rumor fastened on Jaw Naw Ay and his two friends? I could not account for the obvious dislike of these men for Johnson, nor for his antagonism toward them.

But things had gone wrong, and I knew I had to lay the real blame closer to home. I could not blame Johnson — the fault was actually mine. It was I who had divided a group of Karen. If Cad Way's people had expressed the desire to meet in their own village, that would have been the time to encourage and facilitate such a division. But I had been the one to make the suggestion. Though the Christians went along with it, it was my plan. Yes, I must be blamed for the stop and reversal in church growth in Cad Way's village.

I had violated one of the principles of indigenous church growth: I had made a suggestion, knowing fully that the Karen personality of our day and place would accept it without argument. (Thankfully, the day would come when Karen leadership was strong enough to question and veto missionary suggestions.) My action meant, for that day and stage of church development, that it wasn't just a suggestion, it was a decision — one that governed the course of development of that fellowship of believers. With my one infringement I had rendered them voiceless and had taken away their self-government.

It was their own action that had been bringing them as a group across the fields each week to meet with us in Maw Dta. It was at their suggestion and invitation that I had held special household meetings in their village between Sundays. The best picture of initiative was that often, after Sunday morning service in Maw Dta was over, one from Cad Way would invite the entire fellowship to have a second meeting in his home. Then, with a train of bobbling umbrellas shading us from the sun, we would snake our way across the fields. At times there were close to one hundred people walking along for this second Sunday morning service. That second service never originated in my thinking. That was indigenous church life.

I tried to rekindle that initiative within the now still and voiceless men of Cad Way when I asked for their wish. Would they prefer to go on meeting in their own village or to rejoin the group in Maw Dta? Their indifferent response "It doesn't matter" would teach me, as theories learned in Bible school never could have, just how dangerous government of the church can be in the hands of foreign missionaries.

Now all I could do was pray for rain — the blessing of God to reclothe our scars with fresh growth and life. If the promise of nature was true, our blackened hills would soon be green. But what of our blasted and burned church fellowship? Would it grow again? The scent of water had caused the man Maw Dta to grow again after forty years of stagnation. But our cut-down church family had many who could read and needed to drink deeply of that water. We needed a *long* season of rain.

Not long after I got home, Jaw Naw Ay came quite openly to our porch and asked for a private conversation with me. I am sure he knew Nancy Guy would not grasp what was said; as she was still a language student, his very nervous speech pattern was most difficult for her to understand. But two of his cousins were living with us and he knew that whatever they overheard they would broadcast. So we walked down to the empty church, and sitting on the church steps (a bamboo ladder) in full view of anyone and everyone, and yet having complete privacy, he began to tell me what he was planning.

Let me say here that all of Grandfather Maw Dta's children and grandchildren are very good-looking. Visitors to the village have been amazed at how many of the villagers are beautiful. These are almost all direct descendants of Maw Dta. Like all his cousins, Jaw Naw Ay had beautiful, clear-cut features, large dark eyes, and was tall for a Karen and well formed. But his expression was absolutely vacant and his voice was so empty of emotion that I could not really tell whether his opening remark was an accusation, an attack, or just a plain statement of fact: "You know I killed Keddy."

Gulp! In a strange, quivering voice, I agreed with that comment. But Jaw Naw Ay was not angry that he was being talked about as a murderer. Nor was he going to try to clear his name or seek revenge on those who had told. In a flat, empty voice, he went on to tell me that he planned to give himself up to the Thai police, but he did not want to die. Jaw Naw Ay, who had once hated the church and the gospel, now wanted the church to pray for him!

The break from silence to open talk and united prayer of the church family began a work of healing for us. I do not know that our prayers did Jaw Naw Ay all that much good, but they certainly were a help to our own fellowship. The deep distrust and bitterness, the blaming and excusing, began to disappear. With blame now openly placed, there was a real spirit of forgiveness. The village seemed to feel that Jaw Naw Ay was ill and that imprisonment was about the best thing that could happen to him. Without some kind of punitive treatment, they reasoned, he could not manage his personal burden of guilt. They also knew that the jails at Maesod and Maeramard, though miserable places, were used for opium addicts and often helped those who suffered withdrawal symptoms. Three hundred Chinese opium addicts, in fact, had been moved from Bangkok to Maeramard just a year before and were now all out of jail and useful members of society.

We knew it would be a terrifying and miserable experience for this young man; for at best, the physical discomfort would be tremendous and he would be frightened by a language he could not understand and by prison procedures that would keep him wondering what to expect next. Yet this would still be the most helpful experience we could envision for there was another possibility that most of the village feared. I was told that often when the Karen or other tribal men were arrested and taken off to be put in prison, their families would never see them again. Any attempt to trace them would always end at a shallow grave somewhere off in the rain forest not far from the footpath. If the police involved could be located, they always gave the account that the prisoner was shot while trying to escape, and who could disprove their word?

It was no wonder that the Karen did not readily turn to the Thai legal system for justice. In that day the central government had not yet become concerned for justice in the frontier lands beyond reach of roads or telephones. Certainly that sort of thing no longer happens in Thailand, where now even the remotest tribal village has a voice heard by those in government.

Thai police came into the village the very day Jaw Naw Ay talked to me, and I do believe that his intention was to give himself up right then. But the men of the village persuaded him to wait and allow some of them to escort him to the courthouse in Maeramard. This doubtless saved his life, and it showed the concern of the village for him. The men of the church were concerned for the salvation of his soul and for healing and forgiveness in his personality. Though he did pray a penitent's prayer with Jaw Lu, his brother, no one really felt that his crippled mind had taken in very much.

Jaw Naw Ay was not kept in jail very long. Nancy and I felt certain that Pa Gu Der had paid a bribe to have his brother-in-law released. That seemed so wrong to us. Raised on the teaching that bribery is corruption because it "blinds the eyes of the wise and perverts the words of the righteous," we were appalled at the thought of a Christian paying a bribe. But bribery was not considered to be wrong by Thai or Karen. Bribery was so basic to all business transactions with the Thai that the Karen really did not know how to go on without it. It would be years before Christian Karen would begin to talk of bribery as being improper or unfair. By that time Thai Christians would also be refusing to engage in bribery as a function of business, often to their own financial loss. And along with the Christians there would be political and media voices raised denouncing this ancient practice.

In Pa Gu Der's mind, I'm sure, it was right for him to pay to get his brother-in-law released. But Jaw Naw Ay was released before he was even properly cured of opium addiction. He then felt guilty, not only about the murder he had committed but also of the great shame and cost he had brought to his family. Pa Gu Der would have done better to have paid the police to keep him longer.

Throughout the months immediately following the murder, Mu Lay Bpa had been taken again and again to Maeramard, our closest police station, for questioning. Eventually he was taken to jail in Maesod to await trial. This was a dark time of trouble for Mu Lay Bpa, during which he came very close to doubting the love and care of God. But an amazing thing happened which ought to have given him fresh faith as he experienced the Lord's awesome help. Even so, I'm afraid that his frustration blinded him for many years to the extraordinary blessing he had received.

When Nai Promma, the Thai Christian, heard that Mu Lay Bpa was in prison in Maesod and would be put on trial for murder, he immediately went to the authorities there. Nai Promma had once served in the police force for several years and so knew the legal procedures and the language necessary to be an advocate for his Christian brother. He also owned large rice fields and property in his village. His house was a valuable teak structure, and he owned many oxen and water buffalo. All this property he was willing to sign away as surety for Mu Lay Bpa, and he immediately got this brother released from jail. The two men had only met a few times, but Nai Promma recognized Mu Lay Bpa as a brother and had no doubt about his innocence or faithfulness in keeping police regulations while all of Nai Promma's property was in jeopardy.

Those regulations, however, were to rub and irritate Mu Lay Bpa in the months to follow. He had to report for questioning repeatedly . . . until his fields were overgrown with weeds and little of the grain could be harvested. It looked to him like his family would experience hunger in the year to follow. Of course, I would have shared with them — all nine of them! — but then, in God's perfect plan, Nancy Guy came, needing a teacher. Teachers' fees were very minimal in those days, but this still came as a gift from heaven — for Mu Lay Moe taught Nancy.

After those months of questioning, official suspicion passed from Mu Lay Bpa to others, and at last to Jaw Naw Ay. Yet surely the greatest help God could give had already been experienced through Nai Promma. It was a miracle of cross-cultural body life: one part of the body supplying the need of another part of the body. Had they not both been a part of the

Lord's body here on earth, Thai Nai Promma would have despised Karen Mu Lay Bpa.

Throughout the days of multiplied problems, Nancy remained a silent partner. She listened to conversations and my translations of conversations. The problems unfolded and changed from day to day. If she did not approve of the way I handled or did not handle the problems, she never revealed it by so much as an expression. This may seem a small thing, but I am sure it was not an easy time for Nancy; for like most missionaries she is strong-minded, and comes quickly to opinions and decisions. She must have been very convinced that she was not qualified to judge across cultural and language barriers. Had she questioned every action, voiced opposition to every course taken — that would have been the straw that broke the camel's back. Instead, she encouraged.

The church of Jesus Christ often appears to be divided, almost shattered beyond repair on the local visible level. But beneath the visible is the hidden work of God, joining into one body all those who belong to Him. Through this time of trouble, when the infant Karen church appeared to be falling apart, God was fusing together an assortment of people. Our backgrounds, our cultures, our languages were so diverse. I cannot imagine a course of training that could bring together a Scotswoman, an American, many uneducated Karen of the hills of Thailand, sophisticated and worldly-wise Karen from the delta of Burma, and solid northern Thai who are isolated within their self-sufficient farming community, to be formed into one vital unit. The tensions that pulled us in different directions only revealed how inseparably we were bound to each other. We were not a structured organization but rather a living organism.

Chapter 15

Behind the Scene: A Different Story

If you had visited Maw Dta in the years before I took my second furlough, you would have been impressed that the church was vibrantly alive. A new church building seemed to be the heart of activity and life in the village. One Sunday our bamboo chapel had been so crowded that a support beam under the flooring had cracked in two, sending a part of the congregation slipping and sliding down the tilted flooring. How fortunate that they were seated on the floor, and that the church was just three or so feet off the ground! No one was hurt; and instead of concern that drastic repairs would have to be undertaken before another meeting could be held in our little jungle chapel, there was a hilarious atmosphere. We would have to build a new and more substantial building. The church family had talked often of their dream of erecting a teak building to the glory of God. But though we had been taking offerings each week with just this thought in mind, our church treasury held a sum that would hardly pay for a wooden frame. It looked like it would be years before we could afford to build.

Then one day word came that a building in the Thai village about two hours' walk away from us had been struck by lightning. This was felt to be such an evil omen that no one would live in the house. Though Buddhist Thai are not supposed to fear such signs, Thai Buddhism in up-country villages is not really far removed from animism, and the Thai were as much slaves to fear of the spirit world as were the Karen.

The owners of the building could neither use it nor sell it; then they finally remembered that Christians were not supposed to fear the unseen world. They sent a delegation to see if we would be interested in buying their unlucky building. They told us how many boards there were in the building and of what size they were. Then they went on to tell us that the building had a tile roof! We expected the price to be "out in outer space," and almost collapsed when we heard that it was just one thousand *baht* ($50.00). This was a few years before teak soared in price, but even at that time it was a ridiculously low price — and was just exactly what we had in our church treasury. You can gauge the level of my faith when I tell you my first thought was, "Surely, something must be wrong! Perhaps many of the boards were damaged and burned by the lightning!"

A group of Christian men were chosen to go examine the building. Walking together across rice fields and through the woods, they marveled at how the price was just what we could pay. And it sounded as if the number and size of boards were exactly what we needed. This wonder swelled to praise when they found that the house was in perfect condition. They learned from neighbors that it was only a radio antenna that had been struck by the lightning, but the entire house had glowed with a ghostly radiance for several seconds. The men decided on the spot that this was the provision of the Lord and we must buy the building.

The church family worked together to take down the house carefully so that none of the boards would be damaged. Several who had oxcarts helped bring the huge posts and supporting beams to the village. Even women and children helped carry the fragile tiles packed in straw. The boards of the flooring and walls were scrubbed in the river and lovingly sanded until the beautiful grain of the wood stood out.

When the boards were ready, the Christian family joined before daylight in a service of praise. Then the digging began for the deep holes where the giant poles would be erected. Before sunset the frame was up and silhouetted against the glowing evening sky, and we could see the shape and imagine how our new house of worship would look. It was a simple design, with walls that extended only high enough to keep the toddlers from falling off, yet not high enough to shut out the breezes. That open space gave us a scene more glorious than any stained glass window, for flowering trees behind the pulpit area framed a view of the distant purple mountain ranges of Burma.

Village life did seem to revolve around this new building. Though a teacher was paid by the Thai government to come and teach the children of the village, obviously the two-hour walk from his town was enough to discourage him and he was seldom seen in Maw Dta. So Wa Paw, once thought to be retarded, taught the children to read and write Karen, count in Thai, and use Thai currency. Though many Karen families of our area still never used money, roads and commerce were moving nearer all the time and we wanted to prepare our people to meet civilization's challenges with at least the ability to recognize the money of the land. Of course, it was that new church building that was used as a country school five days out of the week.

Our own home was used as a schoolhouse in the evenings when older young people came home from their fields. Da Paw, the bossy one, was the main teacher for teenagers and some in their early twenties who now wanted to learn to read their own language. Each evening just at dusk they would gather, having worked all day in the sun. They had hurried home to bathe in the river, prepare and eat supper with their families, then they would come in groups of friends to study. It was fun! It was encouraging and so exciting to see the young people attracting their friends to fellowship, challenging each other with their desire to read the Word of God, and finally, sharpening each other in the pursuit of God Himself and the desire to know Him.

On Saturday night, joined by some who had walked hours from the hills, the choir met to practice for Sunday meeting. All of this sound and activity would impress any visitor that the church was alive and well in Maw Dta and the hills close to us. But appearance is not always a perfect representation of reality. An example of that was always before us. Dee Paw had become quiet after the death of Keddy, her fiance. To those who did not live with her, her serene smile and faithfulness in the work of the church made her appear as an unworldly saint. But we and her family knew she was desperately unhappy. Hidden behind high cheek bones and almond-shaped eyes that caused her to appear serene and contented was a misery that was heartbreaking. Many young men had come to visit her, and, in Karen custom, made it known to her and her parents that they desired marriage. The next step should be a visit between the parents and a formal proposal made by the girl's parents — that would be Mu Lay Moe and Mu Lay Bpa — to the boy's parents. But since none of the boys were Christians, Dee Paw had not entertained for one moment any attraction for any of them.

Younger Christian girls were getting married, and in the eyes of the hill Karen a girl bypassed marriage only if she had some crippling disease in body or mind. Dee Paw could no longer count the times she had tried to answer prying questions. She had tried to convince so many that she truly had no disease, but rather that she could not unite her life with one who did not love and serve the Lord. Dee Paw was now in her twenties and appeared even older. She was fast becoming an outcast in the eyes of her own hill people. Though she looked serene and contented, she was deeply unhappy.

As Dee Paw's appearance belied reality, was it possible that the picture of Maw Dta church life was also misleading? Though the activities of the church family presented a picture of vibrant life, I knew that beneath that surface there were problems and tensions. There were disappointments and deep unhappiness for some in the church family. With Jaw Naw Ay's imprisonment, most Christians put behind them their feelings of guilt by association or their anger against all related to the killer. But Johnson found no release from his own frustration and bitterness, and could not be really close to any of the church family. However, did his feelings of alienation really start with Keddy's murder?

Not long after Jaw Naw Ay gave himself up to Thai authorities I took a trip to teach and encourage a hill village where there were just a few Christians. One of the pastors from Burma was visiting at the time, and I invited him to go along with a group of young people accompanying me on the climb. I thought this was a great opportunity for the isolated family to hear a voice other than my own opening up the Scriptures. Unfortunately, his voice ran on along other lines. He lectured them to clean up their homes and their village, to acquire education and sophistication that would make them an attractive community to Karen still in spirit worship.

As far as I could see, they were already an attractive community. When the family had first come through in faith and given a testimony to their heathen neighbors, the village was just preparing to move to a new site. This is the common practice of hill farmers after they have worked the hillside area close to their village and now have to begin clearing hill fields several hours' walk away. They move the entire village. A hillside can be cleared just once for hill rice, and it is years before the big trees grow back, cutting off the sunlight so that the dense undergrowth dies away. Then once again a hillside can be cut down and burned off, ready for hill rice. So as this village was ready to move, the village elders met and announced to the Christian couple that they were not welcome to move with the village. They would have to separate themselves and move to some place other than the site chosen by the village.

Massey had explained that the village elders hoped by this decision to force the Christian couple to forsake their new religion and turn back to the old way. No one thought that the family would dare to live alone in the great rain forest. There was real danger from wild animals (the second son of the household had killed a huge tiger their first year in their new home) and from robbers; and without the help of neighbors, illness and accidents could be fatal. And, of course, for those under the fear of demons, the jungle was alive with dark dangers. The village decision was really a mark of their concern for this couple, an indication of their hope that the couple would be restored to them as a part of their unit of spirit worship. That the Christian family chose to live alone in the jungle, just an hour's walk away from the place the village chose, was an indication of their love and deep concern for those families that had always been their neighbors. The Christian couple could have chosen to move into Maw Dta, but they wanted to be as close to their old neighbors as would be allowed.

The first few months in the jungle rain forest alone without neighbors did not see them turn back to spirit worship, but rather it was a time when the older sons of the family came to strong faith. Two nephews moved in with them and also became zealous in their faith. Though they were many hours' walk away from us, it became routine for all the young men of the household to walk down to Maw Dta on Saturday evenings. They would stay for all of Sunday, leaving early Monday morning to walk back to their home.

As the family grew in faith and it became obvious to their old neighbors that they were not going to turn back to the old way of worship, three households from their former village asked if they could move into the valley clearing close to this Christian family. These folk had not yet broken from spirit worship. They were still held in the grip of fear of the demons, but they wanted to live close to and work with the Christian family. It seemed to me that this family group was just about as attractive as anyone could be, for they were attracting families away from the very grip of Satan.

The pastor from Burma could not see the attraction that had drawn the other families to live close to this Christian family. He judged that their language was ugly, their standard of cleanliness low (it *is* hard to get clothes really clean when you must depend on a trickle of water piped by bamboo joints from the spring above the village), and he considered the manners of the family beneath contempt (the words for "thank you," "please" and "excuse me" were completely lacking from the hill vocabulary).

I was sorry that this seemed to be the burden of the message that this guest pastor brought to these people who had really so little teaching. But I was more than sorry when he aimed his guns at the unsaved neighbors. The neighbors in the valley had attended most Christian meetings held on the Christians' huge open porch. When any from Maw Dta visited the village, these folks who were not believers not only attended our meetings but always invited us to eat at least one meal in each house. We were thrilled with the chance to sit with them, to listen to their plans and hopes and disappointments, and really get to know them. So, of course, it was no surprise to receive an invitation for the evening meal from one of these neighbors when we arrived in the village with this pastor from Burma.

Seated on the floor, we ate out of a common curry bowl, and the pastor remarked that the curry was not salty enough for his taste. Now that was perfectly correct in Karen culture. I've often been present when there was good-natured argument about whether a curry was salty enough or hot enough or had enough liquid. So, in accord with hill customs, the lady of the house handed the pastor a handful of rock salt. He should have just stirred the rocks a few at a time into the liquid, tasting it all the time with a bamboo spoon until it suited his taste. But he immediately became offended. He was insulted that she should hand the salt to him, so he began to harangue her.

"You should first pound the salt until it is fine grains, then you should salt the curry yourself," he scolded. "At least you could use a spoon to hand the salt to a guest. To hand over a fistful of this unspeakably coarse salt is so rude." His eyes raked her now trembling hands, admittedly grimy, and on and on he went. When he finally spoke of the fact that her hands were not clean, the atmosphere in the room was explosive.

A few moments later, the pastor began his second lecture of the evening. This was to the effect that the family should have tied up their dogs before they set out food for guests.

The first time I ate in a Karen home I was terrified of the mangy dogs that nosed around, closer and closer to the ring of people eating off the floor, but I soon grew to appreciate them deeply. I could not only toss behind me all the bones and have them disappear before they could hit the floor, but also all other bits of the curry that I found impossible to swallow could go by the same way of the Karen garbage disposal. No one could ever know that I was not just tossing bones as was everyone else.

Since the visiting pastor did not need to have a place of disposal for chicken heads or feet, or a knot of intestine, or singed skin of field rat, he had only contempt for the snarling, fighting dogs. He expressed that in no uncertain terms. Regretfully, that particular household never came to the Lord. Almost immediately the father of the family went far to the north of Tak to join a cult and soon after sent for his family. They were a people obviously unhappy with spirit worship, and with hungry souls were seeking a better way. I do not doubt that that pastor, whose emphasis was perfecting attractiveness to win the lost, repulsed them right away.

The next day he went on to display to me that his ideas of evangelism and the commission to take the news of salvation to the lost were so different from mine or the Maw Dta congregation that only the most surface fellowship was at all possible. We were seated on the Christians' front porch and this pastor was teaching two Maw Dta girls who went with us an alto part to a familiar hymn. Two elderly women from a nearby village came to visit and were fascinated to learn that this man was a pastor from Burma. They knew that there were villages across the border just like their own that had become Christian over a generation ago. Those villages had been spirit-worship centers with customs just like those of our own hill area, so these women had questions about how that change of religion had worked out. Had the spirits retaliated in some way? Were most of the babies stillborn or deformed? Did mothers die in childbirth? Was there drought, flood, famine or pestilence?

That the pastor might find these questions a bit trying to answer I could understand, for he must have been meeting the same questions day after day. But refusing to answer any but the first of their questions, he then turned his back on them and continued to sing with the very uncomfortable young girls.

The Christian mother of the household where we were visiting and I did the best we could to answer the questions, but it was not our answers that these two women wanted. They wanted the experience of the pastor to be told firsthand. I sincerely felt he had gone to the limit of rudeness in refusing to answer the women.

When they had gone, I asked him why he had turned from those two — who might have come to salvation if he had been more patient and kind in answering them. He was so glad that I had put it that way for it gave him an opportunity to explain something to me that he had been wanting to say. As an experienced Karen pastor, he knew that you did not really want too many of that kind of person in your congregation. They were not only dirty and ignorant, but were so elderly that you would never be able to influence them to change. You could make no appreciable change in either the way they looked or thought. You wanted the young that could be taught a standard of cleanliness, who could be taught to read and sing and take part in community programs, and who would present your group before the world as attractive.

I was not attracted! If Christ came to seek and to save only those who could be made to be attractive in this world, then there were a great many hill Karen who would never qualify for salvation. But then, if attractiveness is the qualifying factor, this fellow from Burma did not qualify to my way of thinking!

Could it be that beneath Johnson's more kindly disposition there was this same reaction to the hill Karen of Thailand? Was he repulsed by all that he could not change to match the culture of Delta Burma, schooled by the British and evangelized by America?

Over a year after Keddy had been shot, Pa Low told me that Dee Paw now wanted to marry Johnson. Neither Nancy nor I could be comfortable with this thought. Johnson was not at all settled in Thailand. That he really despised the standard of living was becoming more and more apparent. Though we were sorry for Dee Paw, who had in the past year come through such horrifying and heartbreaking experiences, we could not forget that Johnson spoke of a fiance waiting for him in Burma.

When Johnson came and told me that Grandmother Maw Dta had approached him to make a marriage agreement, it was obvious that he was shocked and really quite frightened. Grandmother told him that he had encouraged the girl to feel that he cared for her. Now the only upright thing to do was to marry her. When he tried to find out just how he had encouraged her, he was dumbfounded by the reply, "You have given her your laundry to wash several times and have allowed her to wear one of your shirts that she has washed for you. And this very moment there is a bundle of your clothing in her keeping!" This last was obviously the crowning proof that Johnson had singled out Dee Paw for his attention.

Johnson was completely bewildered when he tried to figure this out. Yet had he tried at all to adjust to the culture of the hill Karen, had he really considered that there was a culture with some rules and values, he would have found quite early on that it was an accepted stage of courtship for a girl to consent to do washing for a young man whose attentions she did not wish to repulse. The keeping and wearing of his clothing all had significance in the Karen thinking. They had and wore possessions in common. Her washing for him symbolized her willingness to serve him in their home. And the wearing of his clothing symbolized her willingness to have him provide her clothing and material needs. Every Karen in the village except Johnson thought his giving his laundry to Dee Paw over and over again had exciting romantic significance. When Dee Paw appeared wearing one of Johnson's shirts, the marriage was as good as announced as far as Maw Dta and our neighboring villages were concerned. Johnson felt that he had been trapped; but in his talking about the situation I felt that all of his disgust and horror was aimed at Grandmother Maw Dta and not at the girl herself.

Nancy and I strongly advised Johnson to go home to Burma for a vacation. It would mean at least three months away from the village, as much of his travel would have to be on foot. He would doubtless see the girl he called his fiance, and talking about all this to his Christian family would surely help to clarify for him his own feelings. Though I would not have chosen for him to come back to marry Dee Paw, I was determined to keep my opinion to myself. I was hoping that a vacation at home would open up for Johnson an entirely different life. Surely God had a plan for this young man, I thought, and he would have the gifts needed to fit into God's plan.

Johnson told everyone that he was going for a vacation to visit his family. He had everything ready to go, and this time he had done his own laundry! He planned to set out early in the morning, and the day before he was to leave he borrowed a gun to go hunting. It was a homemade gun, and the bullet he used was also produced in the village. Something went wrong with the gun, and with the first shot fired, the bullet exploded in his face, badly burning him. When he was led to us, sobbing and blinded and in great pain and shock, I was so thankful for Nancy who quickly took responsibility. Efficiently she went to work to clean him up and dress his wounds. But she was just in the process of taking over the medical work. As a language student, she had left most of the nursing and all of the stocking of medicines to me, and I had continued to stock only what I knew how to use. So Nancy did not have all she would have chosen to have to treat eyes burned by gunpowder. She was most concerned that we get Johnson to the hospital in Maesod. We sent a runner to try to find out if Wilf Overgaard and his jeep were still in the Maesod area as they had been just a few days before.

Nancy gave Johnson the strongest painkiller we had, but we knew he would have a miserably painful night, and with the pain and shock there could not help but come to him the fear that he would be blinded.

It was our habit to wake up early in the morning when the

village girls began to pound rice, and we would each have an hour or two in our own rooms before there would be much coming and going in the village. It was an uninterrupted time to read our Bibles and pray. It was our time to get direction from the Lord; to get comfort and challenge and nourishment for our souls from His Word before we were called on to give those things to others. We were always awake at least an hour before we had any conversation together. However, I was not surprised when Nancy called me about five o'clock that next morning. She felt we ought to go and check on Johnson.

With our flashlights we set out across the deeply rutted oxcart path and through the weeds to the little bamboo house the church had built for Johnson and another young man from Burma who had come to live with him. When we called, there was no answer, but there began a loud sobbing that caused us to think that Johnson was awake and in pain. Where was Ca Ro Bpa, the young man who should have been with Johnson and caring for him in his helplessness? We went on up the bamboo ladder to the porch, and flashing our lights into the dark room, we gasped with shock. Dee Paw was there, sobbing over the body of Johnson. But as we entered the room, thinking we had come upon a scene of death, Johnson awoke with a start and cried out to know who was there.

"It's all right," we answered, telling him who we were and that Dee Paw was also there with us. But Johnson, startled and in pain and fear of the great darkness that blinded him, was almost in hysterics. Nancy quieted him and questioned him about his pain and when he had last taken pills. Silently, she was thinking and planning what was best to be done about his physical condition, but I was thinking about the scene we had come upon there in that dark morning. What could it mean? Where was Ca Ro Bpa? How did it come about that Dee Paw was there alone with Johnson? All that I could know for sure was that the situation was so against Karen custom, something was terribly wrong.

Dee Paw's sobs continued as we wondered and planned. Suddenly the door was thrown open. There had been no sound of approaching feet, but then bare feet make little sound. Now suddenly there was sound and light as a lantern was plunked down on the floor. Grandmother stood there in the doorway, almost yelling her alarm. Had her words been curses or obscenities, they could hardly have been more shocking.

"This is what is going on! This is how you would deal with my granddaughter! You would have her here with you, ruining her name, taking her face, and then you would just leave her. You would go back to Burma and leave her ruined behind you!"

It was a tirade that would doubtless have gone on and on, but her eye caught movement in our corner and she came to a gasping halt. Nancy and I felt sick about the plot that we had come upon, and I heard my own voice seeming to come from far away. "There's nothing wrong here, Grandmother. We are here, too."

Obviously, that was the last thing Grandmother wanted. She had counted on the appearance of evil to force Johnson to marry Dee Paw. Somehow, Ca Ro Bpa had been maneuvered out of the way so the two could be discovered alone together. Obviously, in their culture, this situation was all that Grandmother needed. The village, outraged, would have forced a shameful wedding.

The truth was that they *had* been discovered alone together, but it had not been Grandmother that was able to uncover the compromising situation. In the Lord's plan, He led Nancy and me to get there first, and we were not about to force such a conclusion. As Dee Paw never did do anything except weep more and more loudly, she could hardly be coached into any part that Grandmother had designed for her. The noise of Grandmother bursting into the room alerted the neighbors, and soon the room was full of those with concern for Johnson. Grandmother, in silence that was as loud as a scream, turned her back on us, pushed her way out of the room and left.

Wilf Overgaard did come that morning with his jeep to take Johnson to the hospital. Because Dee Paw never left Johnson's side, Grandmother never had a chance to question her. How thankful we were for that, for then it would have been Dee Paw's word and not Grandmother's that would have forced the marriage on Johnson. I felt certain that even if he were a bit attracted to the girl, he would never be able to forgive her for such a deceitful trap.

It was obvious that Grandmother was consumed with hatred for us in the days that followed. Then she summoned us to her house. Almost all the adult Christians were seated there, wondering what was about to happen. This was not a worship service we had been summoned to attend. Grandmother had called us to denounce us and to claim that I had usurped her rightful place as head of her family and leader of the church. I was silent, absolutely stunned by the venom of her attack. When I could speak, I gave some sort of answer. I'm sure it was not clever or even particularly spiritual, but I do thank the Lord that it was not angry or sarcastic, caustic or self-excusing. If I had attacked Grandmother in any way, I could have torn apart the body of believers and left wounds that only eternity could heal. I do not think that that encounter took on the guise of a showdown between Grandmother and me, though that is what she wanted. By rather ineffectively asserting that no one could take her place as mother of the clan, and that she had great responsibility in that she had great influence in the church, the spotlight was put on Grandmother all by herself. A village who had been studying the Word of God now looked at a woman who had long claimed to be a Christian, and in the light of the Word of God they found her wanting.

Johnson returned briefly to visit Maw Dta when his eyes were healed, but as we expected, a visit to Burma would show him where his heart truly lay. And he would put Thailand and Maw Dta behind him. But Dee Paw was left with a hurting heart, and I have no doubt that the ones who were once leaders in Cad Way's village hid disappointment and hurt behind their indifferent attitude. And how many others had been made to feel unwanted and unattractive? Only the Great Physician could heal by His continued invitations of love. Only He could see and heal the hidden hurts and reveal to them how important they were to Him.

But I could pray: "Father, fence us in from those who despise the hill Karen, whether they be Christians or unbelievers, whether they be Thai or Karen from Burma or foreigners. Let this newborn church grow for a time without crippling judgment and ridicule of outsiders." And suddenly I realized that Nancy and I no longer thought of ourselves as outsiders. The scorn that burned the Karen burned us too, for we were part of them.

Chapter 16

Christian Stretch Marks

In preparing to leave for my second furlough I was acutely aware that I would be committing an inexperienced fellow worker, Nancy Guy, to oversee a church family in need of teaching that, at her level of language study, she could not yet give. How good it was to remember another inexperienced language student whom God stretched to minister to the growing Thai church in Maesod years before. I felt my experience in Maesod had left me with stretch marks on my soul. Well, now I would trust God to stretch this second Nancy. Maw Dta was in need of love and physical help that would exhaust every resource Nancy possessed, but I could not shield her from this experience. In fact, I knew that were her language more advanced, were her strengths and gifts even greater, then doubtless the tests would be greater, for He would not let her think that she could cope or manage. He was still Lord of the harvest and the Lord who stretches His laborers to show the elastic expansiveness of His grace.

Probably Nancy's most tricky situation of that year would have to do with Ca Ro Bpa. Johnson, in moving into Maw Dta, had invited Ca Ro Bpa to come across the border and share a bamboo house with him. Ca Ro Bpa was a man twice widowed, yet scarcely thirty years old himself. His mother was sister to Grandmother Maw Dta, and his father, who had been dead for many years, had been a pastor. Though Ca Ro Bpa had never lived outside the cultural boundaries of the Christian church, he certainly knew what it was to be outside the boundaries of real body life. His own testimony was that he was wild and willful as a young man, and only in his first marriage did he make an effort to act as a Christian. When he had three tiny children, his young wife died with what seems to have been cholera. Ca Ro Bpa was bitter against God and against the local church that seemed deaf to his pleas for help. He could not be both mother and father to his tiny children, and he made his own situation worse by turning to drink. His in-laws then stepped in to take the three children. As they were still in the grip of spirit worship, the church family condemned Ca Ro Bpa for not keeping the children to raise within the faith. Ca Ro Bpa reacted, blaming the church that he could not keep his children.

There is a story of a time when there was no money to buy milk for the baby and Ca Ro Bpa took his need to the local pastor, knowing that the church had a Benevolent Fund. But the pastor sent this young man away with only a lecture. The pastor feared that the money would go for drink for the father instead of for the baby. Bitterness and resentment were piled up on both sides. Ca Ro Bpa rejected the church and the church rejected him.

Shortly after this Ca Ro Bpa had married a second Christian girl, willing to accept him in his rebellion. She was killed in an accident in the forest when their only child was just a few months old. This child, too, Ca Ro Bpa turned over to unsaved in-laws . . . and turned back to the wild friends of his bachelor days.

That Johnson should ask this young man to come and live with him was a testimony to Johnson's heart concern for his bitter and rebellious friend. The Maw Dta church family joined Johnson in his faith that the bitter spirit of Ca Ro Bpa would be healed and sweetened by the Spirit of the One who was despised and rejected by men.

In the months before I left for furlough there was much evidence that God was dealing with Ca Ro Bpa. Often when I had given Johnson no choice but to come along with me and my retinue of children on short trips, Ca Ro Bpa would come along too. At first Johnson would just listen as I told Bible stories, using picture cards, to the fascination of hill groups who had never before seen pictures or ever heard of Jesus, the Son of God. Soon I turned the story-telling over to Johnson, only coming to his rescue when the locals did not understand his Karen, and only limiting him when he wanted to tell some tear-jerker story not from the Bible and having no gospel application. To my lasting embarrassment, I let him tell one about a poor, stray puppy without home or loved ones to whom he likened the Savior, rejected by men. But I was unmovable when it came to a story about a miserable, ugly old woman who only required seven kisses from a royal prince to turn her into a beautiful maiden. I bet he had an incredible application for that one too, but my stomach just wasn't strong enough to take it.

In those very trying little battles I had with Johnson, Ca Ro Bpa seemed to understand my point of view, and in conversation on porches when the story time was finished it was often Ca Ro Bpa who would pick up the evangelistic thrust and carry it on.

When I left for furlough, Johnson was away because of his wounded eyes, but Ca Ro Bpa was still in the village. The awkward position was that the church family responded to Ca Ro Bpa in a way that they did not respond to Pa Low. In theory, Pa Low, along with Nancy, was to minister to the church. But Nancy found that most often the Christian families turned to Ca Ro Bpa. Nancy had no desire to veto Ca Ro Bpa's ability to minister and wanted his capacity to communicate the gospel to sharpen and grow. But the situation was all complicated by money. Out of the amount Johnson had received — and that amount varied from month to month according to how much I received — he had shared with the young man who made his home with him. Now without Johnson, Ca Ro Bpa was without financial support. He could have cleared a field or taken a job logging, but more and more in the church family were hinting that they wanted Nancy to pay Ca

Ro Bpa to become pastor. Though she and I were an ocean apart geographically, we were not at all separated in our feelings in this matter. It could not be right to promise any financial help to Ca Ro Bpa. He was in no way eligible to be a pastor at that time.

Later I would learn of the strain of those early months of my furlough. There were weeks when Ca Ro Bpa waited for Nancy to meet his financial obligations. The church family was calling on him to conduct meetings in their homes and fields, and the young people counted on his help in leading the choir. Though Nancy was more than generous, she could not in conscience take on his full support. Nancy tried to treat Ca Ro Bpa just as she did Jaw Lu or Mu Lay Bpa and the others who could be called on to teach a lesson from time to time. But it was finally put to her that Ca Ro Bpa ought to be paid.

There was no doubt that Ca Ro Bpa was musically gifted, and there was no doubt that he could be a help in many ways to the Christian church because of his Christian background, but he was not qualified to be a pastor. There was still a bitter spirit, and we had never seen any note of repentance for the wasted years and dissipated strength of his life. And, unlike the Christian men of Maw Dta, we had never heard him commit his life to the Lord.

It was an impossible situation. With her limited ability in the language, Nancy made a statement to Ca Ro Bpa that was absolutely true but which sent him into a frenzy of revolt, and led a good part of the church family to follow him and have a separate Sunday morning meeting in one of the Christian homes. Nancy wanted to state that Ca Ro Bpa was neither qualified to minister the gospel (having never studied, how could he really teach those who wanted to study?) nor did he show forth the qualities of a minister. Stated tactfully, I believe that Ca Ro Bpa just might have been able to accept those two statements. But when you are still a language student, you can only speak bluntly. So Nancy spoke bluntly and told Ca Ro Bpa that he was not worthy.

"You are not worthy" — I have heard him say this of himself

a dozen times since; but hearing it as a judgment from Nancy caused Ca Ro Bpa to explode and shatter the peace of the church.

Nancy was away from the village that Sunday morning of the crisis, so she did not see when our new teak building was almost empty nor hear the sound of singing from the "church split" in the bottom of the village.

By that evening when Nancy was back in the village and in church, most of the ones who had attended the rebel meeting of the morning were so uncomfortable that they were sheepishly returning to the church building for the evening meeting. Nancy had barely had time to hear of the second meeting that had taken place in the morning when it was time for that evening meeting. But even a few moments of feeling that you have spoken the words that led to a church split is too long.

Nancy was reassured that God had everything under control as she watched the church fill up for the evening meeting. But she could not help but be astounded at how He worked out His control when, the next day, word was brought to her that gunpowder had exploded in Ca Ro Bpa's face and he was totally dependent on her for help. Once again Nancy was treating a burned face and eyes, but this time Nancy could see that though the wounds were painful she would easily be able to treat them with the medicine she had on hand. The troubled young man had day-by-day proof of Nancy's care for him and willingness to serve him.

We all realized later that Nancy had put bluntly into words what Ca Ro Bpa felt the actions of the church leaders in Burma had implied: "You are unworthy." He then had split the Maw Dta church, saying in effect what he had said by his actions to the Burma church leaders: "If I'm not worthy, neither are you." But Nancy's care of his burns put it all on a different level: not worthiness, but need. She was willing to serve him in his need. Ca Ro Bpa doubtless saw that no matter how wild a drinker a father might be, Nancy would never refuse milk to his baby — though he suspected that she would be sure to give milk and not money. Nancy's nursing not only brought healing to Ca Ro

Bpa's face, but also to his heart and to the Maw Dta family.

Ca Ro Bpa was just a member of the church family, worshiping and helping with the other men, when I came back from furlough. And his testimony was that he truly came to know Jesus Christ as his Savior in those months I was away. With his new wife, number three, Ca Ro Bpa was working a field and seemed to be putting the Lord first in his life.

I returned to find an air of expectancy among the Christians. The church was once again finding that it had the message that was needed, and there was unity and helpfulness among the church family. Nancy had made blunders in language and culture, but the reaction to her was radically different than the reaction of the hill Karen to the three evangelists from Burma. For Nancy's mistakes were only surface — a wrong word spoken or crazy answers given when she misunderstood a situation. On the level of what Nancy felt or intended, she always revealed the heart of a servant. No Karen could long be in doubt that Nancy was their servant, and the result was a church not only being served, but serving. There was an outreach of Christian service on all sides.

Men cutting hillsides for the year's rice planting found that men working the same general area would walk an hour or more just to question them about what it meant to be a Christian. Women carrying peppers or searching for pigs to buy often found that they were walking along the forest trails with others who had heard how they had broken from spirit worship. Their eager questions gave the Christian women the opening to share the gospel.

Men who went off to work for a season in the logging fields found that the fact that they had become Christians was the most interesting topic of conversation. Vast areas of mountain slopes, hills and valleys were covered in a logging season by the Karen and their elephants, employed by first foreign and then Thai government companies. The overseers chose and marked the giant teak trees for cutting, and the teams of Karen felled and gathered the huge logs, using their elephants to drag the heavy trees through the rain forest. Later, logging roads would be cut for trucks to haul out the stacked logs, but just one rainy season would see the roads washed out and a dense growth of underbrush would obliterate all marks that man had ever worked those hills. These logging camps became the scene of evangelistic witness in the evening when the heavy work was done, and the men and elephants rested around the blazing bonfires.

The fantastic changes in the lifestyle of the Maw Dta and other hill village Christians brought men from as far away as seven days' walking journey to inquire about this change. I saw, in the growth of the church, that God places men who have come into a right relationship with Himself into the position of authority in the world. It is as sure as gravity that men released from spirit worship and given the right to call God their Father will advance in cultural achievements with a progress that is astonishing.

Thai peddlers had always come selling to our village, and it is their report that before so many villagers turned to the Lord they needed to come only once or twice a year. They brought thread for weaving, matches, a bit of kerosene, perhaps a can of fish, some fish hooks, safety pins and some gaudy jewelry — and that was a reflection of the hearts' desires of Maw Dta. That is where we were in culture, hygiene and cleanliness. But after the turn to Christ, the Thai sellers suddenly found that they had a market. They reported that no matter how often they came, they could not bring enough laundry soap, bath soap, toothpaste, shampoo, bath powder, combs and toothbrushes. There was an endless demand for kerosene as readers multiplied and evening was the only time they had to pursue their new love of reading. Pencils, paper, envelopes and notebooks were ordered constantly. All kinds of foodstuffs were in demand. Clothing and shoes were brought and displayed on our porches. And the sellers went home at the end of the day with empty baskets and full purses. Or more often than not, baskets full of peppers or onions exchanged for manufactured goods.

When Thai officials came to lecture in the Thai village

across the fields from us on how to get better yields from our rice fields, it was Karen Christians who crowded around to ask questions. Men who had all their lives known only one meager rice harvest a year now experimented with the new miracle rice, and planted soybeans or garlic in between their huge harvests. The hill farmers planted a corn that the government bought for export. Suddenly we were not only a market for Thai produce but had a market for our own produce.

Bamboo houses were replaced with teak, something not allowed in spirit worship. And a village that straggled along beside the river took on a more orderly appearance as pigs were fenced in to keep them out of the new gardens.

A globe I had brought back from furlough fascinated the villagers and young people who had thought that the world was flat. They traced with their fingers the route my ship had traveled in bringing me back from America. A village that had exploded in a frenzy of fear at an eclipse of the moon, beating on tins and pots and shooting guns to scare away the great toad who was thought to be swallowing our light, experimented now with a flashlight, tin pans and that globe to understand the shadow that caused the eclipse.

It was just a few months after my return that Nancy and I were staying with a family in Dry Creek Village. We listened that evening to the world news in Karen that was broadcast from Chiengmai and heard of the moon landing and the first walk on the moon. After the broadcast was over, it was fascinating to listen to our Christian host and hostess trying to explain what it was all about to their unsaved neighbors. These new Christians not only listened to world news on their tiny transistor radio each evening, but Jaw Lu had also explained to them about an eclipse and what caused the moon to appear to wax and wane. All the neighbors of this Christian family feared the uncertainty of the moon. The only thing they knew for sure was that each month a moon grew to full size and then began to fade away until there was nothing left. There was nothing permanent about a moon. Truly the moon pictured the insecurity of all of life — nothing was sure except death and replacement.

The Christian man Pa Tha Yay, with great fluency, explained what Jaw Lu had shared with him of the permanence of our ancient moon. His neighbors were having none of that far-fetched stuff. They did not believe the report of the radio, because for them there was no outer space, no universe. In fact, they did not want to hear about the world beyond their own mountain range. For them there were no people of importance beyond their own family groups. The Karen name for themselves is their word for "human." All other groups and nationalities are for them somewhat less than human, not just in vocabulary, but in their estimation.

Pa Tha Yay, who listened to his radio nightly, was even then negotiating to sell his elephant and buy a truck. He figured that the roads were coming closer, and as elephants retreated back beyond the sound of horns and motors and the smell and speed of trucks, his elephant would become less valuable and less usable. Trucks would take over more and more of the heavy hauling and moving that elephants had done for centuries.

Karen Christians were experiencing the truth that God had created the earth a habitable place for man. Men could have dominion over the seasons and riches of the earth. For generations the Karen of the Thai hills had feared the wind, the rain, the sun, the rivers, and even the very soil. They lived in bondage to nature, which they saw as their enemy. The gospel changed all of that until with new eyes Christian Karen looked at a world that was created to serve them. They made the leap from bondage to dominion with no push from us. I saw that there was no way you can keep new converts from animism from advancing in education and culture. It is part of God's plan and man's birthright. Who needs to teach it or make a crusade of it?

It was at this point of exciting stretch in the Maw Dta church family that I did something that the three workers from Burma had done. I looked back to my own country and Christian experience to find the pattern of how the church should move out.

I longed to see the Lord calling into His full-time service some of our young people. And out of my own background I believed a call to serve was a call to prepare, and thought in terms of formal Bible schooling.

Nancy told me that when Johnson returned to Burma he had taken two of our young men to attend Bible school there. She was informed that it was the teaching staff of the Bible school who helped these two boys get false papers and false identity cards, and that it was the pastor of the largest church along the Burma-Thailand border who had claimed them as a part of his Burmese church family and acted as character reference for them, though he had never once met them. There was no way that Nancy and I could accept this dishonesty as a way of life acceptable and glorifying to the Lord. We felt we could have no hope of even the most shallow of spiritual teaching from this connection with Burma.

Back before I left for furlough, at the time our teak church building was being erected, we had guests who all got down on hands and knees and helped to dig the holes for the building's huge posts to stand in. These guests were a foreign missionary and a Karen pastor from a denominational convention connected with a different mission working to the north of us. They had come a roundabout way by car, crossing the mountains between Tak and Maesod, instead of walking for two weeks south along the border as most Karen would have to do at that time. I do believe they came merely to see and have fellowship with the Karen church in our area. The Karen pastor had ministered to us at the Wednesday night service while the church was not yet finished, when we had to step along support beams where the flooring had not yet been laid, and was a very real blessing to all that heard him. But these men left behind them a situation that would change the profile of the Maw Dta church.

There was a school for Karen established now in the northern province of Chiengmai. We were told that though there were classes given in hygiene, agriculture and cottage industries, most of the hours of classroom study were given to Bible. Though this mission was of a denomination and not connected with WEC or any other interdenominational mission operating in Thailand, we did not know of any important doctrinal difference that would cause us to feel that their school had to be off bounds to our young people. And just hearing of this school was as the carrot to the donkey. Every young person wanted to go north to Bible school.

Now back from furlough, because of my own regard for education and because of the prodding of some in the church family, I was involved in the decision that two girls would go to Chiengmai to Bible school. These were the two eldest daughters of Mu Lay Bpa: Dee Paw, who had been engaged to Keddy at the time of his murder, and Wa Paw, who had once been thought to be retarded. We did not choose these two. They desperately wanted to go themselves, and their parents were willing to let them go although they could ill afford to lose their help in the fields. That willingness of the parents is probably the main reason why it was these two of one family who went. Though other young people desperately desired to go, their parents could not spare them from the fields. So we began writing back and forth to the school staff and the missionaries concerned with the Bible school, and it was agreed that these two sisters would go for the next school term.

I wish I had known more about the culture and the character of the hill Karen of Thailand before I made that decision. And I wish I had also known more about the ways of the Lord before I made that decision, for the need of that hour and that place was for *stretchable* people — not just people enlarged by formal schooling, but people who would be able to go on and on stretching by the grace of God to meet the ever-expanding need in the hills.

Chapter 17

Dominion, Not Confrontation

Many hours' climb beyond Maw Dta in the high storm-swept hills, a young married man named Maw La Pay became demon possessed. The details of that day of terror are a confused puzzle of crisis and emotional reaction for him and his tiny village of just seven houses. But the story is told of how it took all the men of the village to restrain him from harming his young wife and baby, and they could not restrain him when he threw himself off a steep cliff. I have seen the place of his fall and realize only a miracle kept him from being broken in body, if not killed outright. But the report given by all present was that he was not even scratched or bruised, and so the weary men of the village struggled on to subdue him until night, when the destructive spirit left him.

Maw La Pay was unbelievably tired and terrified as he listened to the account of what he had done that day. And there was no hope for him in all his familiar world. All he could look forward to was repeats of this day just past, until his terrified family and neighbors would have to take his life to protect themselves. He wondered even then if the circle of loved ones and friends about him were already planning his death.

At this point he remembered Paw Naw Tha, the man and his family thought to be so unattractive by the pastor from Burma. The story of how they had escaped from the claims of spirit worship and were worshiping the God of creation had reached far out into the hills. Maw La Pay had heard, but had given the story no thought at all. Now it arrested him. Surely if anyone could help him, it would be this group.

Maw La Pay earnestly tried to persuade the men of his village to go with him immediately to this distant village. But they would have none of it. They were not only bone-weary with the day's exertion, they were each one terrified of being off in the dark forest with this man who could at any moment become possessed of a wild and terrifying spirit. Their friendship and love for this man whom they recognized as leader of their village was now no match for the fear and dread that closed them against him. Not a one would dare to go with him. But Maw La Pay had now become convinced in his mind that Paw Naw Tha was the place where he would find help, and his longing for help was stronger than his dread of the lonely, dark trip. He would go alone.

For hours he stumbled along the black forest paths. Often he ran with the sound of feet pursuing after him. Or was that just the pounding of his own frightened heart? The strange noises of bamboo, their giant fronds seeming to cry and wail in the wind that bent them high over his head, sent him almost out of his mind with terror. Was that sobbing, weeping thing coming along behind him . . . or was it he himself?

It was early morning, with just a trace of light along the mountain tops that rim the valley of Paw Naw Tha, when Maw La Pay stumbled into the village clearing. The villagers, just stirring, heard the lumbering, staggering runner and his shuddering, gasping breaths. Had some wild beast been pursued into the clearing? Would they hear the trumpet of a rogue elephant or the cry of a wildcat hunting this inhuman thing roaming beneath their houses? Soon they made out that the hoarse cries were human and they were pleas for help. The Paw Naw Tha family quickly arose, kerosene lamps were lit, and the bamboo ladder was lowered into place. Maw La Pay found that helping hands were lifting him up the rungs of the ladder onto the porch. A fire was built up and blankets were brought, and the comfort of the familiar hot food stilled his shuddering sobs. At last Maw La Pay was able to tell his story and plead his need.

Perhaps this is the place to say something about a Christian church surrounded by evil spirit activity. I knew that every man in our group had been trained as a spirit doctor. Some, as Mu Lay Bpa, had experienced strange powers that they could not control. Every spirit doctor knows something of demon possession. Frankly, and surprising as it may seem, when such men came to declare their faith and wanted me to pray with them I could never think of them any differently than I had thought of the innocent children who accepted the Savior's love. I never prayed with anyone as an exorcist; I did not cast out any demons nor did I take any daring stand against the spirit forces. I just presented the gospel to those men and presented them to the Lord for His complete work of salvation.

I once heard Robert Mackey, then international leader of WEC, speak about two words in Luke 10:19: "Behold, I give unto you power over all the power of the enemy." He explained that the first word translated *power* ought really to be translated as *authority*: "I give unto you authority over all the power of the enemy." Mr. Mackey went on to maintain this is not just a quibbling over words, but makes a real difference in life and practice: for power meeting power means confrontation, but authority meeting power means dominion. Who cares how much power the enemy has? We do not need to trouble ourselves about that. We have been given authority over *all* of his power!

In the early days of the Maw Dta church I could not have put that thought into words, but I saw it acted out again and again in the lives of those delivered from the power of the evil one. I marveled that there did not seem to be any fear of their former masters. Dominion and not confrontation seemed to be the hallmark of the first men converted from the blackness of spirit worship.

The Christian family of Paw Naw Tha did not give Maw La Pay some formula to use to annul spirit power. They did not talk or think about the power of the evil spirit world at all.

They simply presented the gospel. They told Maw La Pay of a Christ who withstood every temptation, and having proved Himself to be impervious, who took our sins upon Himself and died for us. In His dying, He set us free from sin and death. They spoke of salvation, of union with God, and Maw La Pay listened and believed. No doubt when he heard the word *salvation* he equated it with deliverance from the demon world. Others equated it with help to overcome opium addiction, the slavery of spirit taboos or some other ruinous habit that had brought them to despair. But as all believers have found, salvation reaches men where they are and puts them into the position where God can work in their lives to deal with their problems.

With the removal of sin's penalty, God could deal with Maw La Pay as a son and give him authority over all the power of this enemy. Maw La Pay did not have the vocabulary to speak of his position in Christ, but he knew he had found the help he needed and he was free from the expectation that he would again be attacked by the demon of the past day. He did not expect conflict, but took dominion for granted.

Maw La Pay's astonished village was alerted to his return when they heard his cheerful whistle. In just the time required to send boys off to bring in two elephants grazing in the forest and tie on their baskets, Maw La Pay had not only explained about the help he had received in Paw Naw Tha but was now on his way to bring back foreign women who would teach his village. With his accustomed authority, he commissioned different ones to go in different directions, inviting friends and relatives in other villages to be present when the foreign women arrived.

At the other end, we knew nothing at all of this story. We were taken completely by surprise when a man we had never seen before got up at the end of a Sunday morning meeting and began to speak. Maw La Pay has a rather fierce expression, and that day he was badly in need of a haircut. Nervousness made him sound quite angry with us. At first I really wondered what we had in our midst, but his story quickly stilled every other sound in the restless auditorium. And when he ended by pronouncing that he had brought elephants to take Nancy and me with him to his village, we were excited to fall in with his plans!

Fall was almost literally the right verb to use to describe the end of that trip. At last, at the end of a long day of travel, we came to the village just at twilight, and though there were just seven houses in the jungle clearing, there was a great crowd to witness our clumsy descent from the elephants. Trying to move our paralyzed and painful legs that had been cramped in one awkward position all day and then step from the constantly swaying, shifting elephants onto a bamboo porch that was also on shaky, decaying legs, is no mean feat.

The village was already building new houses an hour's walk away. These old houses would be left to rot away in the next rains, and those rains were already upon us.

After a quick bath in the tiny stream, we were fed hot rice and curry made from some unmentionable kind of meat. I always hoped that it was not monkey or rat or cat or dog. And as always, I was thankful for the Karen automatic garbage disposals snarling and snapping just behind us!

And then we had the floor and were to explain just what had taken place in Maw La Pay's life, and how men in bondage to Satan could be set free. Along with giving such an introduction to the gospel, we were to show filmstrips. While on furlough I had purchased through the mail a little projector that plugged into a flashlight. With spare batteries and several filmstrips on the life of Christ, His teachings and miracles, and a series on His death and resurrection, I felt I had enough to use for several nights.

This little invention was particularly made for the use of missionaries and is put out by a Christian group, Mitchell Art Products of Los Angeles. I am so totally unmechanical that I panicked when I first saw what I had ordered through the mail. But I believe it was Mr. Mitchell himself who answered my SOS and explained in layman's language just what to do. None of this "positive and negative" rigamarole for the likes of me!

He had to speak of the black clamp and the red clamp. On my next furlough, Mr. Mitchell even went so far as to make a battery case from a file box when I wrote to order some parts for my machine that had worn out or been broken. He obviously could see from my letter that he was dealing with one who *needed* help.

We showed two or three strips that evening, and with the explanations needed it was a long and exhausting meeting. But — would you believe — they just kept asking for more until we had gone through the whole works and all the strips we planned to use the next three nights! We hadn't a filmstrip left, and no voice to speak of, either.

In between the different filmstrips, Nancy and I had introduced the people to one gospel song, "What Can Wash Away My Sin?" But we had made a great error. We first taught them the words of the first verse and then we thought we would sing it through for them, so that they could hear the tune. Well, they obviously felt that a tune was the last thing they needed. When Nancy and I began to sing, the entire room began at the same time. If we sang louder to try to get our voices heard above the din, we found the room was also singing louder! They enjoyed the singing to the fullest. We thought it was the most awful ruckus we had ever heard, and we learned right there (if we ever had any doubts) that we certainly did not have forceful personalities. We would have been outweighed even if there had only been one Karen. Nancy would say, in her purring Scotch accent, that we had the sort of singing voices that couldn't be heard behind a wet newspaper!

It was well into the middle of the night when we squirmed our way to the wall and lay down — without a blanket, and just using our spare clothing as a pillow. But the meeting was far from over. Aw Pay Moe had accompanied us from Paw Naw Tha, and her presence had been a great help throughout all of the meeting. Now she was answering questions about what happened when she and her family became Christians; now her testimony was being questioned and examined and remembered.

I vaguely recollect hearing a discussion about the "head pig" and how it ought to be killed or sold or gotten rid of some way when a family became Christian. Now, that is just the sort of thing I really did not know anything about, but Aw Pay Moe knew that in every house there is a female pig dedicated to the evil spirits. As long as that pig or one of its female offspring is alive, a weak Christian can be tempted in times of trouble to believe that the spirits are wanting to claim their own. Temptation comes continually to turn back to spirit worship, and as long as the head pig or one of her female piglets is still alive, the door is there, opening the way to darkness.

Years later we watched and puzzled over a family who had seemed honest in their profession of faith and desire to follow the Lord. Though their church attendance was erratic, and we began to wonder if the father was not on opium, we felt we could not judge that they were not real believers. But after years of professing faith, their eldest daughter became so ill that she was beyond the help of medicine. Suddenly the family turned back to spirit worship, and it was revealed that through all the years of professing faith they had kept the line of the head pig alive. The way back to spirit worship was always there for them. They had secretly carried out ceremonies that dedicated pigs to the spirits as the old pig died or was sold off. In spite of their verbal commitment to Christ, they had always kept open a way out of that commitment.

That would not be allowed to happen in Ga Dru Sa Key. The village was too small. They knew all about each other. Nothing could be hidden, and they discussed this long into the night. If they accepted the God of Maw La Pay, the God of those filmstrips they had just seen, then there must be a total canceling of the old way and there would be no way back. There was enthusiasm and strong attraction, but there was also fear and holding back as the evening's conversation advanced. In spite of the real spiritual battle raging in that bamboo home, I believe that our exhaustion would have caused both Nancy and me to sleep soundly . . . but we were not allowed to do so. A bony finger poked between our ribs every once in a while to check if we were asleep, and the request now and again to repeat that beautiful song assured that we did not spend an undisturbed night.

The next morning Nancy and I were inside Maw La Pay's house. I do not remember if we were alone, but I do know that most of the members of the family were out on the outside porch and their conversation came through the open weave of the wall. "Now that we have all decided to worship the Lord, the first thing we must do is to tear down our spirit shelf." That came as a complete surprise to us. "Gwee Lee, go tear it down," the voice continued.

Now we had been too overwhelmed by our reception the night before to be able to get anyone's name. Who was Gwee Lee? The door burst open and in marched a tough little girl of nine or ten. We remembered that she had been introduced to us as an orphan who was living with Maw La Pay's family. She attacked the high shelf with great vigor, though she could hardly reach it. I was out on the porch immediately, trying to stop this. All I could think of at the time was that this fearful job had been passed on to an orphan child. Did this mean that the others were fearful and unwilling to take the consequences of the act and so passed it on to an innocent child? Maw La Pay did not let my agitation stop the proceedings for even a moment. If his reaction could be translated into English, it would have gone something like this:

"Calm down, relax, everything is under control. We know what we are doing. No one is taking advantage of Gwee Lee. You think we are despising Gwee Lee to use her in this way, but that's not it at all. We are showing the spirits that we despise them when we choose a child — a girl, an orphan — to destroy their shelf. All our lives the spirit shelf has been the center of worship in our home. Great respect has been always shown to the high shelf: no one can sleep with feet pointing to this shelf. When offerings have been made in this house, it was, at first, always my father-in-law who attended the shelf. After his death, the honor fell to me. Children are never allowed to touch the shelf, and a woman can only touch it if there is no man to act as priest. This morning we are Christians. Would it be right for us to show such respect for the shelf today?

"*No!*" he answered himself. "Gwee Lee, take it off and burn it!" And the child staggered down the steps of the porch, the heavy burden of the only wooden structure the house had contained on her shoulders!

Six out of seven houses burned their spirit shelves that day; and early the next morning, as the day was just breaking, the seventh household made its way up the hillside away from the village with all their household goods on their backs. They feared to be part of this village "gone mad."

I do not know just what I would have suggested if it had been left to me to do away with the spirit shelves. I don't see any New Testament pattern of just how one eliminates the paraphernalia and attachments of the old life, but Maw La Pay's answer let me know that he knew a great deal better than I did what was involved in the burning of the shelves. And there is no doubt about it, they were ridding themselves of bonds that represented the demonic hold on their lives. Maw La Pay understood just what they were being delivered from and how wide that deliverance is.

With the conversion of the six households of Ga Dru Sa Key, we suddenly had a branch congregation that would have to be ministered to. Our elephant trip home from that first visit quickly gave us some understanding of what an impossible task we had. Nancy and I began the day by encouraging each other that that trip would soon be over and the medieval torture of an elephant ride behind us. Brushing off wet leaves and dozens of caterpillars that were in our hair, on our faces, and down the necks of our clothes as we passed through a forest being devoured by these gruesome worms, we reminded ourselves that in just a few more hours we would be home and could have a bath in our own bathroom. We could get *really* clean instead of taking the token wash we had been having in public streams under constant observation, where there was always great interest to see if we might drop the bath skirt we used to wash in.

As the day progressed, the skin wore off us at every point where we rubbed against the *howdah* basket on the elephant's back. Bites from mosquitoes, flies of all sizes and bugs of every description became swollen and itchy and sore, but we continued to think in terms of soon being home and getting all those bites and sores cleaned up and ointment put on them. We would surely have no bad infection, for the day was so cool that the elephants did not do their usual trick of sucking up the filthy, muddy water from every puddle they passed and spraying it all over their backs. This is no doubt very cooling for a hot elephant, but that "bump" on the back that is the passenger becomes drenched and dripping with scum, making every tiny scratch become a festering sore.

I thought the tropical downpour that started just after we passed Paw Naw Tha was a suitable finish to the day's horrors, but it was just the beginning. After the experiences in the caterpillar forest, we had gotten lost and wandered around in the forest until we were sore enough and itchy enough for a lifetime. The driving rain was not the finish. The wind came in such gusts that our umbrellas were turned inside out and it took all our strength to get them closed and put away beside us in the howdah. The sharp bullets of rain then hammered us, soaking all the way through our clothing and leaving us feeling bruised by their force. We had to quickly put away our glasses because they were so wet and streaming with rain they were no help to our vision anyway, and we were literally afraid that they would be swept off and broken by the force of the rain.

Even without our glasses we could see that there were streams in places where there had never been any course of water before. Coming down the steep mountainsides were now great shooting waterfalls. What had been tiny streams had suddenly become rivers. Then we came to our own river. It was such a shockingly wide expanse of water that had it not been moving at such a rate I might have thought it had turned into a lake. No longer were the rocky bottom or any boulders visible. I could make no guess at how deep the water might be, but one glance at the faces of our elephant boys and we knew that we were in real trouble. Looking at the white churning water carrying huge clumps of bamboo, whole trees and logs, I could understand why they were now so pale.

Nancy Guy, on the larger elephant, had a young girl who had joined her in the basket as they started down into the water. "Please hang on," the girl begged again and again. "I am," a terrified Nancy proclaimed. The girl had to forcibly prove to her that though she was hanging on with a death grip, she was clutching both hands only to the handle of her umbrella! To be fair, I must admit that Nancy's terror was not really for herself but for me on the smaller elephant. And she was right, for my smaller elephant was in for trouble in the deep, rushing river. All I knew was that suddenly the basket tipped over, the swift water flowed over me, and then it was all right-side-up again, and the elephant was climbing out on the other side of the river. However, we were probably one hundred yards downstream from Nancy's elephant and the spot for which we had been aiming.

Nancy saw the elephant flounder and crash onto her side, her legs swept out from under her by the current. And in that moment that the basket was under the water she wondered, "How do you explain to your co-worker's parents that their daughter has drowned in a river that usually only comes up to her knees?" The elephant boys were terrified of the many crossings that lay ahead of us before we would reach Maw Dta, so they detoured up a steep hill where there was no path. It is doubtless a testimony to our state of shock that we were too numb to even get alarmed at dodging huge wet branches, bending ourselves to avoid getting swept off the elephants, or bending the branches when they were so low they could have swept off the baskets, moldy ropes and all. This is always the story when you are not on a clearly marked elephant path where all dangerous branches have been cut back. And if the elephant insists on charging ahead faster than the elephant boy can cut branches, it is just up to you to be nimble and strong.

Up the steep hill we went, and all I really recall about that part of the trip was that the elephant basket I was sitting in was battered until it could never be safely used again.

Detouring brought us to the village of Thaw Ray Blaw. Here was the house where I had taught reading. The father of the household was shaking like a leaf as he literally lifted us down from our elephants onto his porch. Along with the elephant boys, he knew that the miracle was not that the elephants had crossed a swollen river. Evidently all elephants can swim, and love water. But swimming uses muscles that swell their stomachs (or chest, or *whatever* that part is connecting all their legs), and the expanding muscles are guaranteed to snap the moldy ropes that tie on the howdah. That the elephants had made it across the river without snapping these ropes was all the miracle that any of them were asking for. Once was enough. No one was going to take the elephants into a flooded river again that day.

So these dear friends provided us with warm, dry clothes. They quickly built up their fire and put on rice to cook. How long ago it seemed that Nancy and I had started out the day by encouraging each other that we would soon be home and would not have to look at rice again, for there was a loaf of bread in the kerosene refrigerator, and in our own home we would be able to cook potatoes. What sheer delight! But, of course, that was not to be. For though we were just one hour's walk away from Maw Dta, we did not get home that night.

That hot rice meal served by our hosts at Thaw Ray Blaw was just what we needed, and it was given with the most gracious hospitality. Mats were put down for us as close to the open fire as was safe, and the man of the house built up that fire again and again during the night. I am sure he was terribly impressed with our chattering teeth and the chills that shook us as if we were in the throes of violent malaria. The warmth and safety of that home soon had its effect and we drifted off to sleep with the drumming sound of rain pouring down on the steep leaf roof. Sometime in the middle of the night I awoke. What was the sound that had brought me from sleep? I soon realized it was the quiet that had awakened me. The rain had at last stopped. The roof stretching up steeply above us and lost

An exciting way to travel.

in the shadows of the smoke from the fire was absolutely quiet.

But though the rain had passed over and was flooding the Tak side of the mountains, the river was still a wide, rushing, uncrossable barrier. The elephant boys would not dare to cross it. But it was again possible to detour the river and, we hoped, get all the way to headman Cad Way's village. So after a hot rice meal that morning, we set out on a detour of the river that took all day. Part of the way was down what had been called "an all-weather road," just completed by an Australian construction company. I do not know about Australia's weather, but those surveyors had no idea what "all" meant in Thailand. The water was up to at least six feet on the sides of our elephants and was moving so swiftly that it was hard work for the elephant boys to keep the elephants from letting that current propel them at a rate that would be dangerous for those moldy ropes.

Once at Cad Way's village we were royally welcomed again and our own Christian family made us feel truly at home. Our own house with its privacy, its indoor bathroom and refrigerator with food our foreign taste buds longed for, was just visible across the fields. However, it could have been a million miles away, for it was beyond reach until the swollen river went down.

That flood was saying graphically to Nancy and me that we would never be able to be the helpers, teachers and encouragers that Ga Dru Sa Key needed. Though flash floods do not occur often (our river was flooded and uncrossable six times that year), there were other physical barriers and limitations to also take into account. Nancy would soon be leaving for furlough. And I had recurring malaria, and there were responsibilities that would tie me to Maw Dta. Ga Dru Sa Key was an exciting harvest, but it deserved to be better tended than the care we could give.

Though we did not even discuss it with each other, that flood that kept us from home was causing us to be deeply concerned about the little Christian village we had left behind. But we were not the only ones thinking along those lines. The

Christian men of Maw Dta, who served regularly, teaching in the evening services, leading their friends to the Lord, encouraging each other and discipling new believers, were also looking at the river and the rugged hills beyond, and they were seeing a field "white unto harvest." They would not now sit back and say, "This is missionaries' work." Perhaps they might not have felt that way had we been men or had we equipment and transport that would have made our job easier. But they looked at us and looked at the harvest, and that was all they needed to convince them that they were needed. God was calling them into a deeper involvement in His work, a time-consuming involvement: an involvement that would cost them in strength, and mean smaller hill fields cultivated and a margin less of this world's gain and comfort. We did not enlist their aid, but *God did*.

I only wish I had seen all that this meant before the two girls left for Bible school. I felt, as I am sure the men of Maw Dta felt at that time, that schooling would polish helpers for them in the outreach to the hills. For we were all looking at that whitened harvest field and taking it by faith, as those who have dominion.

Chapter 18

A Family Affair

With Christians many hours' climb away in the hills, we needed the help of the men of Maw Dta. We already had men well qualified to fill the office of elder, and these were the men who were the ones responsible for most of the distant hill communities of Christians. They already had concern for the ones they had led into life and were willing to go when fellowship and encouragement were needed. Now they were willing to add Ga Dru Sa Key to No Day Bau, Dtra Dtraw and Paw Naw Tha. They could go and teach, they could pray and spend hours talking about problems and circumstances until the newer Christians came to see their situations with a Christian perspective. In effect, they were already shouldering much of the work of elders, but as yet they had no official recognition.

Nancy and I felt that their labor of love ought to be given recognition. We felt they were ready for all the honor that goes along with the burden of service. So we again took up a thorough teaching of I Timothy chapter three. There is nothing obscure, nothing hidden or mystical about the qualifications for elders. They are intensely practical, and instead of comprising a higher and separate set of rules for the few, they are a spelling out of the life that pleases God. And though they serve as guidelines for every church member, they are law for the ones who would be leaders and examples for the entire church.

When one of the church members remarked, "If that is

what an elder is, then we already have three," we were thrilled.
The church member then went on to list the three that we had
been thinking of as elders for some time: Jaw Lu, Debbie Bpa
and Mu Lay Bpa. Later, when in discussion it was seen to be
possible to have the men who had come from Burma as Maw
Dta church elders, Ca Ro Bpa and Pa Low were added to the
list.

In a sense we were not scriptural in the way we gained
elders, for what we did was simply to recognize the spiritual
leadership that was already there. Paul appointed elders, and
the accepted understanding of the Greek wording of Acts 14:23
is that their appointees were then approved by a show of
hands. Though Nancy and I could have appointed elders,
Karen men would certainly have felt that we were usurping
authority over them. Though we would have appointed the
very ones recognized by the church, the Karen men would
never have been comfortable for women to so direct the
church. And to the very day of this writing, the idea of voting
by a show of hands is so foreign it results in a complete fiasco.

I do see, too, that it would really be unsuitable for me
personally to appoint an elder, for I always see the church men
through a motherly emotional evaluation. I want them all to be
mighty through God. I saw Cad Way as a strong leader and
coveted that leadership for the Lord. But the congregation was
right in passing over Cad Way when elders were recognized,
for Cad Way's leadership was not a spiritual leadership. As a
government headman and natural leader of men, he would
have had much to unlearn before he could learn that spiritual
leadership is not top position but an in-between position. For a
true elder leads as he is led by the Lord. In the years since, as we
have seen men of strong leadership ability come into the
church family, some have become elders, but they have been at
great disadvantage for they have had to unlearn the aggressive,
self-assertive ways that made them leaders in the world.

Perhaps the most graphic time when emotion would have
governed my choice in the matter of elders, were the choice up
to me, was when one of Mu Lay Bpa's daughters was disobey-

ing his teaching and turning her back on the way of the Lord, stating that she would marry an unsaved boy. Mu Lay Bpa, our eldest elder, our brother in the work, announced that he must resign his position as elder. He had no choice, he said. It was not a matter of what he wanted or what he thought was best. It is just simply stated in I Timothy 3:4 that the elder is one "having his children in subjection with all reverence, for if a man knows not how to rule his own house, how shall he take care of the church of God?" For Mu Lay Bpa and the men of the church, it was a simple matter of obedience to the rule of Scripture. For me, there was nothing simple at all. I was an emotional wreck and would have worn myself out trying to look for loopholes around the teaching. But the church was not following my choice in the matter of elders anyway. (In a very short time, Mu Lay Bpa's daughter had repented and was back into subjection to her father, and I do not doubt that seeing her father's step of humiliation did much to show her how wrong her act of disobeying him really was.)

Shortly after the first group of elders was recognized, a group from Cad Way's village, just twenty minutes away across the rice fields, was baptized. It was Mu Lay Bpa who baptized them, and it was Ca Ro Bpa who led the communion service. A few weeks later a group from Dtra Dtraw, six hours' walk away in the hills, was baptized, and this time it was Pa Low who performed the baptismal service and Jaw Lu who served communion. Starting with the first elders meeting, the men chose who would perform the baptism and serve communion in each place and each time. No man was ever free to act in baptizing converts or serving communion without that group's endorsement.

While the Maw Dta elders were testing their legs in this walk of service, God was working way out in the hills to bring the village of Ga Dru Sa Key into His family. During the first month after the villagers burned their demon shelves, the men of Maw Dta took turns visiting, teaching and encouraging them. And they came back home so encouraged themselves that they could hardly conceal their joy. Often they came back with questions they could not only not answer but would never have thought of themselves. The elders grew as they carried their new brothers onward.

The young people of the church were already helping in other Christian hill communities, and they now also took on Ga Dru Sa Key. We sent them two at a time to stay for a few days in villages where there were new believers. It worked something like this: Two young people went to stay in Dtra Dtraw for two weeks. They took reading charts to help teach the alphabet and reading and writing. They took lots of books, notebooks and pencils for their pupils to practice with. They also had a series of flash cards on the miracles of Christ that they would teach each evening, and two or three chosen hymns that they hoped to help the people memorize. Two others would go to a different outpost of the faith to teach reading and writing, but their flash cards were a series on the parables of Christ and they would teach different hymns than those taught by the first pair. The next two had a series of flash cards that dealt with the arrest, trial and crucifixion of Christ and they had different hymns to teach than those taught by the others. Two others taught a series on the nativity, the baptism, and the temptation of our Lord before His public ministry began. Hopefully, these young people would rotate and each couple would visit every village before the year was out.

Actually, it never worked that smoothly. Illness and pressure of work made it impossible for any pair to visit every place. But there were others who would take a turn or two at teaching. There were other series of lessons from the Bible that would eventually be taught: a series on the life of Paul, one on the life of David, one on Elijah and one on Daniel. And on this base of Bible background the elders could build, teaching the church from the Epistles.

Seeing the needs of such a scattered congregation, we began a tape ministry that would expand the knowledge of the growing church. I do not mean to give the impression that we had found the most effective and authoritative way to church expansion and structure, but we had been given by the Lord a pattern that fit our situation at our point in time and in our culture. It was a family project — older family members helping and teaching the new family members, and I believe that it tied us together in a way that mere organization could not have done.

Since Nancy and I found contemplation of trips horrible, we decided to make it a policy that when we were invited to go we would just go without giving ourselves time to contemplate the trip! I cannot number the trips going and coming from Ga Dru Sa Key and other villages when one or another of the moldy ropes tying the howdah to the elephant became loose or suddenly snapped in two. Once on a steep mountainside we were coming down carefully and I could see down over the head of the elephant boy to a drop of fifty or more feet, almost straight down to the next outcropping of rocks. Suddenly I felt the rope slipping and let out a spontaneous yell that so frightened the elephant she turned right around in her tracks. It was the rope that fastened around the elephant's tail that had snapped. Had the elephant not turned completely around until she faced uphill, the basket would have crashed forward, knocking the elephant boy from his perch. Hearing the experts later considering just what would have happened if I had not terrified the elephant into turning around, the most comfortable outcome that can be imagined for both the elephant boy and myself was broken necks and a speedy death. Anything less than death would have meant many hours of waiting for help to come and make slings to lift us onto the elephants, or tie us to deck chairs to be carried by four men at last a three days' journey to the nearest hospital. But fancy my being such a loudmouth that I could frighten a mighty elephant into making an instant about-face!

I could not count the times when the ropes have gradually become loose and tormented the elephants until the drivers had to find some place for me to get off in order to retie the ropes. On one harrowing trip I was asked to step from one elephant to another so that my basket could be made more secure. That might be high adventure for some, but I am so

clumsy that I can barely navigate on high heels through plush
carpet. For me to get up my nerve to step from one swaying
elephant to another (and they never sway in the same direction
at the same time) is just torture.

On one of my last trips when, as usual, I had to scramble off
the elephant so that a moldy rope could be retied, I watched as
all the bags and bundles packed around me were taken out of
the basket. I then nearly collapsed when a young man who was
walking along with the elephants picked up a red woven bag
that I had been half leaning against and half sitting on — for he
withdrew a menacing looking pistol and tested it, firing it
without doing anything more than pulling its trigger! There
was certainly no safety catch (whatever that is).

"Do you mean that is what I've been sitting on?"

"Sure!" The young man could not see any cause for my
alarm. "Ma Law Pay thought we might need this if we met any
communist insurgents."

Doesn't it just boggle the mind to think what might have
happened if we had met robbers or insurgents? I can just hear
the frantic exchange.

"The gun is in the red bag." My bleated "What gun?" would
naturally be ignored as superfluous conversation, and a barrage of "The red bag, the red bag!" would have bombarded my
confused ears.

But "Which red bag?" was worthy of an answer, for there
were at least four red bags with me in the basket!

"The one you are sitting on," would have had startling
results, I am sure. If I did not then break all records for the
sitting high jump, my slithering around to get off the bag
would surely have resulted in shooting myself or the elephant
in the largest part of our respective anatomies! I know I ought
to be grateful to Ma Law Pay that for my safety he sent along a
gun. I *ought* to be grateful, but I am not!

Yes, I have walked the journey, making it a full two-day
trip. I have done it by spending the night at Paw Naw Tha; but
getting up at dawn and going all day until dark up and down
steep hills in a tropical climate is a far cry from hiking and

camping in the cool climate of North America. I found the trip so exhausting that I was not able to have much ministry when I reached my destination.

The last time I walked to Ga Dru Sa Key was during the year Nancy Guy was on furlough. It was just an hour's walk further to the village, and I was so tired at the end of my long day of walking that I could not move fast when ... *I stepped on a viper!* The young people with me became so hysterical in their screamed warnings that I stopped altogether to figure out what they were so excited about. As they were yelling at me to move quickly out of the way — some yelling at me to jump, some warning me to move back, another frantically yelling me onward — my stopping was the last thing they wanted. But by the time I understood, there it was — a *dead* viper. Attempting to strike me, it had curved up over my instep and bit itself instead. Injecting its venom into that spot, it had poisoned *itself!* It writhed a bit and then lay dead.

I was still not really sure what all the alarm was about. Not that I could not get quite alarmed at any little worm or tiny snake, but the Karen do not usually get excited about anything less than a cobra. However, the young people explained to me as we sat around the corpse of that viper that I would not have been able to walk at all for twenty-four hours. I would have been writhing there on the ground in pain, and our supply of aspirin would not have been a great help.

That experience convinced the Karen that they did not want to be responsible for my walking, so they have always sent elephants when they were ready to have me visit in their villages.

There was another consideration in their sending for me and Nancy Guy when she returned from her furlough in Scotland. They sent for us at their own convenience. Often there are few if any men sleeping in a small hill village. The men are scattered away in fields and the great logging camps. Because the villages are really poor and there is not much of value that could be stolen and sold for cash, they never fear robbers. But with a foreigner present in a village it is a different proposition.

Opium addicts and Thai bandits would surely think that we had money with us or even valuable jewels. The villagers could not afford to have us unless there were several men at home. With their guns at the ready, they were not afraid of any danger that we might attract.

Of course, we were determined to keep going to the hills to serve the emerging church. We would go on foot, on elephant back, and years later as advancing roads reached back into the hills, we would enjoy the luxury of a truck. But from the very beginning of church growth in the hills God was showing us that not only was *evangelism* best done by a mobilized church, so also every *other* ministry necessary for growth and blessing was best carried out by a Christian family, willing to serve each other.

A month after the villagers of Ga Dru Sa Key burned their demon shelves, there were five men of Maw Dta who went to have a baptismal service. The men were each asked to sleep in a different house in order to give the new converts the chance to question them. Jaw Lu told us in amazement that "those people just don't sleep. Why, every time I was just about to drop off to sleep, someone would think of another question!"

Nancy and I could hardly keep the silly grins off our faces as we remembered our sleepless nights in Ga Dru Sa Key. How marvelous! We could remain snug in our own beds, eating our own kind of food, bathing in our own bathroom instead of in the village stream, while Karen men, to whom none of those things expected of them in Ga Dru Sa Key were at all foreign, went to minister. We were almost more thrilled at the elders' growth and eternal rewards than we were at the reports of snowballing church growth.

There was a wonderful story just beginning in Maw Dta at that time that pictured in the natural what we were doing in the spiritual. One day Mu Lay Moe was coming home from the day's work in the fields. Her husband and older children would shortly follow her, and if she hurried she would have the rice cooked for them and a bit of hot sauce and vegetables prepared for the evening meal. But she could not hurry. As she passed one of the first homes in the village she heard the wailing of the funeral cry. Knowing that the mother of that household was just about to give birth to her fourth child, Mu Lay Moe guessed that the mother had died in childbirth. There would be no wailing if the baby were stillborn or lived just a short time — that was too common to even qualify as tragedy. Only if the mother died in childbirth would you hear the funeral wail.

So Mu Lay Moe did not waste time asking if the young mother had died; she knew that to be true. Instead, she called to ask what was of no interest to anyone else, "Is the baby alive?"

The body of the mother was by this time prepared for burial, and the father had already turned from his older living sons and was finding solace in the lying dreams of the opium pipe. As the little bundle in unwashed rags had ceased to cry hours ago, no one even knew if the tiny boy was dead or alive. But yes — in his dark, dirty corner the unwashed baby was still breathing.

Mu Lay Moe knew that the boy would be buried with his mother whether he was dead or alive. As far back as the dawn of history the Karen had realized that without a mother to feed and care for a newborn baby the infant would die. No, that's not really the way to say that, for they had no chance to realize it. Spirit doctors declared that the departed spirit of the mother would come back to claim the baby who had taken her life. And every time a Karen tried to keep the baby born of a mother who died in childbirth, the quick starvation and death of the baby just added authority to the spirit doctor's pronouncement. The idea was never that a mother sought her child in love, but in revenge: because the child's birth had cost her her life, she would claim his life.

I found it so depressing that there was never any thought of love beyond the grave. But then, in Karen culture, it was expected that both mother and child would be born again to never remember or recognize past lives or loves. Even the anger and revenge only lasted as long as the disembodied spirit wandered near the village before it started a new life.

Mu Lay Moe knew all this so she was not surprised that nothing had been done to make this new little life clean or comfortable. She knew that at the first sign of hemorrhage frenzied incantations were begun and that insane pleading with the spirits to spare the mother's life had driven every thought of the child from everyone's mind. In fact, Mu Lay Moe told me later that because of bruises on the baby she thought that he had been literally thrown aside, thrown into his dark corner.

Mu Lay Moe, though a close friend and neighbor, could not go up into that house. The forked branch was in place, and as a Christian she was accounted as much a foreigner as I would have been. A few years before she would have been helping there as midwife and Mu Lay Bpa would have been summoned as a spirit doctor. But now Mu Lay Moe was barred from entrance into that home. The baby, in his nest of rags, was handed to her. And looking down into the tiny face that began to wrinkle up, and with pouty lip outthrust and quivering chin let out a mighty howl of rage at his poor reception into this world, Mu Lay Moe knew that she could not let this baby be buried alive.

"You are a fool," the mourners taunted her. "You claim the mother's son and perhaps she will claim yours!"

If Mu Lay Moe's resolution could have been shaken, that surely would have done it. Although she had many daughters, she had just one son — dearly loved and completely spoiled. As she set off for home with a new son, the mourners were filled with terror and wonder. But the tiny baby did not know that he was being taken from the edge of the grave. Perhaps he recognized the security and comfort of a real mother's firm hold, but he could not know that a large family would all quite happily wait for a long overdue meal while two adopted sisters would rush against the advancing darkness across the fields to the Thai village to buy a can of sweetened condensed milk. And water had to be boiled and cooled for his milk before the family's rice was set on to cook.

Mu Lay Moe knew from the outset that she could not

afford to take that baby. A daughter that was just old enough to work for the first time in the fields would have to be used for the care of the little boy. The canned milk, though not the best kind for feeding the newborn, was the only kind that could be used, for without refrigeration sweetened condensed milk is the only kind of canned milk that will not quickly spoil. However, it was much more expensive than evaporated milk. But on her way through the village with the baby, Mu Lay Moe passed the home of Jaw Lu, her nephew, and when he understood what was happening he gave her the price of that first can of milk. She had taken the child without even the price of one can of milk on hand.

The adopting of that baby meant sacrifice for every member of the family. For years, sisters, aunts and cousins would carry him around and look after him. His aunts would weave his blankets and little red Karen jackets. His new sisters would teach him where his nose was, his eyes, his mouth. He would be taught by his new family to walk, to feed himself, and he would be brought by them to worship and to know the Lord. Jaw Lu's paying for that first can of milk was an example of what would be repeated again and again. I doubt if there was even one poor Christian family who did not contribute at least one can of milk for Pa Say Go. Everyone wanted to cheat the grave, defy the spirit doctors, and step on the heartbreak of their old customs. Claiming Pa Say Go from the grave was their greatest joy.

Surely what Mu Lay Moe's family was doing for Pa Say Go was parallel to what the church of Maw Dta was doing for Ga Dru Sa Key, for Paw Naw Tha, for Dtra Dtraw and Thaw Ray Blaw. Soon, farther out, other villages would be added, and like Pa Say Go they would need to be firmly carried, fed and taught. It was a family project to care for them and serve them. As Mu Lay Moe could not afford Pa Say Go, we could not really afford Da Do Su Tha or Da Ya Blaw or Da Mu Key. All these villages with their wide influence would shortly turn to the Lord. But each of these villages was to be claimed from the very edge of the grave, and each was to become a family project. We were, for a time, a mobilized church, everyone having a part in the caring for our new brothers and sisters. That was a time of exciting harvest.

Chapter 19

The Church

Danger! Men at Work

or

Glory! God at Work?

Early in the morning, long before daylight, the sound of a buffalo horn would echo through the sleeping village. Each owner of a field had his turn to act as pied piper, summoning the workers of the village to follow his horn to help harvest his fields. Most farmers had worked alone to prepare their fields, plowing behind a water buffalo, and all alone mending the built-up walkways through the growing rice. All alone a man could sow the seed that would, when transplanted, cover a huge field. But when harvest time came, a man had no choice: a host of workers was needed to harvest what just one man could sow.

We were feeling that pressing need for harvesters when the time finally came for the Karen Bible School to start classes for the year. Mu Lay Bpa could hardly spare the two daughters he wanted to send, and as a church family we knew that we would feel the loss of these two just as keenly. For Dee Paw and Wa Paw were among our most willing and gifted young people. There was not a group of believers anywhere in our hills that they had not visited, staying days at a time to teach and encourage. They were as willing to help the family that hosted them labor in the rice fields or do laundry in the stream as they were to teach Bible stories. Along with Mu Lay Bpa and Mu Lay Moe, we made a real sacrifice by sending these two girls away for schooling.

It was the season of monsoon rains, and the Maesod road out over the mountains was more often closed than not. Though men did not seem to mind sleeping several nights on the road, it was surely unsuitable for two young women, so the girls were to fly from Maesod. Mu Lay Bpa escorted his girls the day's walk to Maesod and was on hand when they boarded their plane. This was the first time in history that a Karen from the Maw Dta area would fly in an airplane. Mu Lay Bpa was suitably overwhelmed, although he regained his composure enough to give his daughters some parting advice. Remembering Nancy Guy and her experience on the elephant returning from Ga Dru Sa Key, he admonished his daughters not to fear if anything went wrong in flight, but just to hang on tight to their umbrellas. Absolutely typical of Karen humor!

The next year Pa Low's son, Jaw Ooh, and Gaw Naw Hay, a young man from Paw Naw Tha, joined the two girls at the Bible school. And these four would show us how a formal, away-from-home schooling experience would affect our church family. During the four years our young people were away, we wished again and again for their help, for the wind of God was moving here and there, breathing life into the dead. It was the day of harvest. It was a time of joy and responsibility as God was stretching and spreading the living organism that is His church.

One day I was summoned to the porch because two hill men had come seeking me. They had come at an awkward time, but any girl who was living with Nancy and me knew that it never mattered what we were doing; if a caller was from the hills, we wanted to be interrupted. Nancy Guy was away on furlough, so though I was in the middle of washing my hair, I was the only one to receive them. I wrapped a towel around my soaped head and went out. I could easily have felt that this interruption was a waste of time and been terribly annoyed when one of the men held out a hundred *baht* bill and said they had come to me for small change, but I had been among the Karen long enough to know for sure that whatever else they had come for, it was certainly not for change. This was surely just a pretext for these two very shy hill men to call at my house. I knew that back in the hills there was very little use of Thai currency; Thai traders never went far beyond the roads and oxcart trails, so if the men were going to use their hundred *baht* ($5.00) they were going to use it in a Thai town where they could be given change anyway. But I did have enough change in the house that day, so some bills changed hands. Then some information was exchanged.

These men were from a village a day's walk away, but Cad Way acted as their government headman and for all the villages in their area. One of these men was a nephew of Cad Way. "Do you understand what it means that Cad Way has become a Christian?" I asked them. "Well, yes." It just so happened that that is what they really wanted to talk to me about. Cad Way had been telling them of his salvation and his blessing in the Lord. He had been talking not only to these two but also to all the villages under his authority. A bit of conversation revealed that these two wanted to become Christians. They and their families had talked it all over and admitted their faith to each other. Now these two had come and the question in their minds was, would I accept them? They were just simple hill farmers without lands or animals, they had no education, they could not speak much Thai and could barely recognize the alphabet of their own language. As they apologized for themselves, it was readily apparent that they really doubted if they qualified to become a part of God's redeemed ones on earth. But I told them that if, as they listened to Cad Way, a longing had been born in their hearts to experience this same salvation, and if hearing, they had believed Cad Way, that proved they were chosen of God. The longing and the faith were from Him. I think they felt they were the most important men in the world that day; and of course, they were and are.

When I later heard the story behind the hundred *baht* bill that was brought to me for change, I was really amazed at the response of those two men to the attraction and drawing of the Lord. Up until just a few years ago, Karen loggers were paid in rice, salt, whiskey and opium. Only once in a long while were they ever paid in Thai currency. And back in the hills, that money was useless. Men spent their money on Thai clothes and returned empty-handed to their families. Or some did as Pa Yu Ay (one of these two visitors) had done when his bamboo house was being built: he buried his pay under the first house-post to be erected. It was a gift to the spirits, and as a gift it would never be reclaimed. After three years or so the village moved and Pa Yu Ay built a new house. The old house rotted away in the rains and jungle growth. After a few years there was nothing but memory to indicate that a house had ever stood over the site of that offering. But when the two men began to plan their visit to the foreigner, they thought, "We can't go to her without some excuse, some business to transact. What will we talk to her about?" Then they remembered the offering to the spirits, and decided to dig it up and bring a bill to me for change. Isn't it the oddest idea that I would welcome them if they had some business transaction but might not receive them if they just came and told me that they wanted to know the way to be reconciled to God?

Just think of the act of faith and courage as those two men went to the site of their old village. They could not help but believe that demon eyes were on them, watching their every move as they began to dig at the place they remembered the house-post to have stood. I am sure they were jumpy and fearful at every sound: the flute-like piping of birds hidden in the giant bamboo, the echoing laughter of monkeys from their lookout points high on the cliff face that overshadowed the village site, and the strange, almost human cry of the huge bamboo branches arching over them. But with their bare hands they dug down until their fingers felt the old oilcloth bundle. Then they walked several hours to tell a foreigner that they wanted to become Christians. They were Christians already!

Cad Way had given a full picture of the way of salvation and they had believed in their hearts and talked together with their families, confessing their faith and winning their loved ones to that faith. All I had to do was pray with them, introduce them to some Scriptures that would give them assurance of salvation, get them together with the elders who would bear the responsibility of teaching and worshiping with them, and arrange dates for trips to Da Do Su Tha, their village.

In time a cassette player was given to them and teaching tapes sent for them to study. But the first contacts would be personal: Ca Ro Bpa and Mu Lay Bpa, and the young people from Maw Dta and Paw Naw Tha. That very first day the two made plans for an elephant to come get me for a visit to their village. And though I suppose they were pleased to have this strange-looking foreigner in their village (and certainly they made me feel welcome), I could never think of those first trips outside the light of a remark Pa Yu Ay would make after listening to his first teaching tape: "It's so much easier than having you; we don't have to feed it!" I must admit there is something of that thought in my mind when I make tapes for the hills, too. For it is the custom for every Christian or even an interested household to feed you during your visit to their village. Nancy Guy once counted that we were fed rice seven times before seven o'clock in the morning!

We expected that the four who had been sent to Bible school would add greatly to our effectiveness when they returned at school vacation time, but we found that our young people did not come back willing or equipped to do what our churches would require of them. Some things began to show that first vacation time, and they would become more obvious with each year until the graduation of the four. All four really wanted to settle down in Maw Dta and teach the choir! This was actually the least needy group of all that came under our fellowship of churches. In fact, this was the group that was constantly being used to minister to the needy in the hills. For them to be held in Maw Dta to be taught several new choir anthems was just great, except that it would be done at the expense of four or five tiny groups way off in the hills who only knew two or three hymns, a verse or two from John chapter three, and the most surface application of a few gospel stories.

The Bible school students came up with amazing excuses

for not being able to remain more than two or three nights away from Maw Dta. Jaw Ooh feared he was getting a fungus growth under his fingernails because he had to eat with his fingers. He had never eaten with a spoon until he went away to school. Dee Paw found that she got a very upset stomach from eating the hill food. It was exactly the same food she had eaten for the first twenty-two years of her life, and was not really any different from the food being eaten in her own home right then. Gaw Naw Hay suffered headaches because he could not get enough water to drink, for he now had to drink only boiled water — as he had seen pictures of germs in unboiled water. Karen hill homes keep a wood fire going almost all day, but since they are cooking meals and also pig food, it just was not possible for him to boil the water he needed to drink.

The young people had had just enough hygiene education that none of them were able or willing to live in the hills for several years after their graduation. Another problem was that because of their having been taught "cottage industries" (a subject that must have been broad enough to include several money-making projects) all of the young people now equated financial prosperity with successful Christian living and were on the lookout for what could be purchased at a low price from hill Christians and then sold at great profit to the Thai. They had also come to realize from their schooling that the ancient coins that most hill Karen owned were worth a great deal of money. And handwoven skirts, jackets and blankets could also bring a good profit when sold to the Thai. When they were sent off by the Maw Dta church to minister for a two-week stretch in a distant village, we would not only find them returning after just a two or three-night stay, but they came back with shoulder bags full of what they had traded for a few cans of fish or jars of rotten shrimp paste and would hopefully sell for hundreds of *baht*. I cannot tell how much it hurt me to realize that the church that sent them to school was now being exploited by them, and I do not for one moment think that the Bible school staff meant to turn out such products. But they exposed them to a standard of living that could not be achieved honestly from the starting point of those young people without many years of hard work — and the shortcuts were all too obvious to those very intelligent young people.

On the next vacation from school, Wa Paw brought the entire project of the Bible school students teaching in the hills to a screeching halt: she brought home with her a boyfriend whose nickname was "Doll." It was the most fitting nickname I have ever encountered. He was so very pretty — he had the features of a baby doll. The teaching staff had told him not to follow Wa Paw home, but Wa Paw's orders were to the contrary and he came at her bidding.

"We are engaged and will be married in two years' time," Wa Paw informed everyone with great finality while the doll sat behind her and looked pretty.

We sent Wa Paw to teach in just one place that year, and her doll went along too. The next thing we knew, the two most prominent men of that village were on our porch with an account. "They ate out of the same plate!" "They bathed together in the stream!" By their tone of voice and look of face we could see these were things obviously not done, but the manner of the telling let us know there was worse to come: "They stood side by side in the window of my house talking to someone in the yard!"

My immediate reaction was, "So what?" But, of course, I did not say it. I knew we had hit the culture barrier and I was not really able to get the meaning of what I was being told. I soon realized that to eat off the same plate, to share it, was only done by married couples. And even though the bathing place in the stream was in full view of the entire village and both were wearing the prescribed modest bath-cloth, for an unmarried man and woman to so bathe together was just not acceptable. As for standing side by side in the window of the home they were staying in, that seemed to me the silliest accusation of all; but again, it was not acceptable to the Karen. As the affair was discussed in Maw Dta, I found that most of our own people were dreadfully offended that this young couple had walked together side by side up through the village. Jaw Lu proclaimed that he would not walk side by side with his wife of several years. And realizing that the church always separated itself into the men's side and the women's side, families never sitting together, I realized that this was Karen culture and they were not going to accept it being set aside by the Bible school students.

That the village where Wa Paw was teaching wanted her recalled, and none of the other villages wanted her, seemed to me ridiculous. The offense seemed to me so small and meaningless. Our headman, Pa Gu Der, wanted the church leaders to immediately repudiate Wa Paw's announcement that she was engaged and would be married in two years. Prolonged engagements were not acceptable in Karen culture. If the two were engaged then they should be married right now, the headman announced. And it was not to be at the announcement of just the young people but at the considered agreement of parents and elders concerned.

When Wa Paw and the others were graduated two years later, she was still considering herself engaged to the doll. But coming home without him, she became reacquainted with a boy from Cad Way's village she had always known slightly. He was not particularly handsome, he was violently opposed to the gospel, and he would not let Wa Paw boss him at all. There was certainly nothing doll-like about this young man. In no time at all, Wa Paw came to feel that whatever she felt for the doll, it was not love. She wrote, telling him she would not marry him — but she had enough Christian backbone to remain adamant that she would not marry the local boy either unless he committed his life to the Lord. She was utterly miserable and made life unbearable for all her family for almost a year.

It all looked quite impossible, and I don't know who would have given in. The doll still wanted to marry Wa Paw; Wa Paw wanted to marry the local boy as soon as he came to the Lord, but he was unyielding and would have nothing to do with the Lord. All this was extremely foreign to Karen culture. "If that is the way the Bible school teaches young people to carry on, we want nothing to do with it" was the verdict of the adults of the Christian community. Of course, the Bible school did not teach them to carry on that way. The Bible school, run by foreigners and Karen from Burma who had lived in city and not village communities, simply relaxed rules where friendship between sexes was concerned. And because of those relaxed rules, Wa Paw was in no frame of mind to now fit back into a pattern where her mother and father would make the choice of a life partner for her. Wa Paw was making the choices for herself, and she was making a mess of it.

Finally, the local boy was unexpectedly and soundly converted. The entire Christian community breathed a sigh of relief the day that couple was married. "I was afraid we would inherit that doll," Jaw Lu whispered to me when the ceremony was completed.

There was another barrier that caused the Bible school students not to be acceptable to the emerging churches. Schooling was still a very foreign concept at that time. A father trained his son to do all that he could do, and a mother trained her daughters to do all that she knew how to do. All of youth was spent in training under parents and older relatives. And only when the older generation was too old to work was the next generation thought to really have caught up on ability and accomplishment. That you would send young people away to be trained far from the family setup and they could come back expecting to be in authority over the older generation was unnatural and uncomfortable for the hill village and Maw Dta elders. They were doubtless very critical of the young people's gifts and abilities, and the four students felt they were on severe trial every time they attempted to speak or teach. It was certainly not yet time for the Maw Dta area to send their own young people away to be trained for the Lord's service. Those young people had all been a help in the hills before they went to school, and they would never be a help again.

I would judge that our experiment of sending the four away to school was tragic. First, because the school was situated in one of the largest and loveliest of Thai cities — so hill Karen from tiny, isolated villages were exposed to wealth and luxury beyond their dreams. This exposure was ruinous to our four young people. Secondly, the relaxation of tribal customs sent our four young people home deeply despising the control of their elders and in revolt against what they considered outmoded and meaningless conventions of their people. But the third failure was our own and cannot be blamed on the school. The men of the church ought to have foreseen that a training outside the village family setup would bring young people back, not just to help, but rather to teach their elders. Along with the elders, I ought to have been able to guess that this would be impossible for the church to accept at that time. We were not yet living in the age of schools.

We could not look to Burma for workers in our day of harvest. We could not even send our own young people away to have them receive the training we could not give. Obviously, God was hemming us in so that we would experience the truth that He can give gifts to a local body to meet all the needs within that limited group. I kept remembering something I had heard: "Bloom where you are planted." And it spoke volumes to me. We were hillbillies, cut off from the sophistication of this worldly-wise day. Our culture was so uniquely Thailand hill Karen. Perhaps nowhere else on earth are the rules of what is acceptable exactly duplicated. I needed to see that where we were planted the Word of God could cause us to grow — grow strong, grow up into spiritual maturity, grow out into everwidening circles — a multiplying church family.

In spite of the darkness of the Maw Dta hills, in spite of the mistakes of missionaries and national workers, God was building His church. One Sunday after the morning worship service was over, the congregation gathered on the riverbank behind the church where several were to be baptized. As the congregation sang together, those who were to be baptized followed one after another out to meet the elder appointed to perform the baptisms that Sunday. The moving water acted as a mirror to hold that scene against racing clouds framed by high mountains. And born-again people stepped out into the waters to testify that they had chosen to identify for all eternity with the One who was crucified for their sins according to the Scriptures, was buried, and rose on the third day according to the Scriptures.

Looking at the picture of the stream, the elder, and the man next to be baptized, I suddenly remembered a dark room where a baby had lain arched in convulsions, with death just a few moments away. The head spirit doctor sat over the dying child while all the men of the village rimmed the walls of that room with black hopelessness. There was not one adult Karen believer in that room. In that village and in all that mountain world, death reigned. The pictured memory faded as the man to be baptized gave voice to his faith and commitment to the Lord Jesus Christ. And clasping his hands, he yielded himself to the elder to be lowered into the water. Ma Blee Bpa, the father of that child who died years before in that dark room of spirit worship, was now giving visual testimony of his faith.

Ma Blee Bpa had grown through the stages of childhood to manhood under the umbrella of his grandfather Maw Dta's love. But the testimony of his mother Day Zay, who had been to Christian school in Burma only to return to the mountains of Thailand to practice the dark arts of a spirit doctor, insulated him against the power of the gospel. When his first child, Ma Blee, died, his heart was encased in a blackness of total commitment to the powers of evil. When his brother Jaw Naw Ay murdered Keddy, the young pastor from Burma, Ma Blee Bpa had applauded in his heart and hoped that the wave of conversions sweeping his people away from unity in their ancient religious rites would stop.

But the Word of God had at last penetrated Ma Blee Bpa's entombed spirit. It was a scent of water that brought life.

Thinking back to that dark room of death, I could not overlook the missionary there on the bamboo floor. I could feel again the dismay and misery I felt when I realized that the head spirit doctor was the father of two lovely Christian girls. Day after day his daughters prayed with me for their father's salvation. And praying with them was a battle for me, for temptation to doubt that one so committed to spirit worship could ever come to faith in the Lord had to constantly be denied admission to my thoughts. I had to keep choosing faith and refusing doubts. I had looked at the tiny group of believers in Maw Dta and thought, "This is not right. This is not the way to go about planting a church. We ought to start with men. We ought to start with the responsible leaders of the village." But those little daughters of Mu Lay Bpa had held me to choose faith when everything I saw and heard contradicted faith. I could never for one moment relax my guard in front of those children. I could never express doubt, for they were tender and young in faith and I dared not be a voice of unbelief to harm the work God was doing in them. And they were right, of course, for God *did* indeed save the mothers and fathers of those first Christian young people of Maw Dta.

It was a picture of miracles I looked at there in the stream. Ma Blee Bpa was the picture of a miracle of a changed life. And so was the elder who lowered Ma Blee Bpa into the river and then raised him up out of the watery grave, picturing resurrection and the power of an endless life. That elder, faithful servant of the Living God, was Mu Lay Bpa, once head spirit doctor of Maw Dta.

We were a church of miracles. But we were also a church of mistakes. We had made so many mistakes and would doubtless make many more in the days and years to follow. But the meaning of salvation is that God has stepped into history, into flesh and blood, into our situation of sin and mistakes. He can make right what is wrong, light what is dark, and alive what is dead. Because of Jesus Christ our Savior the picture of a tree cut down is also the picture of men and women cut down, and "there is hope for a tree, if it be cut down, that it will sprout again, and that its tender branch will not cease. Though its root grow old in the earth, and its stock die in the ground, yet at the scent of water it will bud and bring forth boughs like a plant." And the ongrowing, outspreading of Christian life is not sustained by just a *scent* of water, but by showers, rains, and then — as our Savior promised! — the flowing out from the believing heart of *rivers* of living water.

Martha Hill - 3/27/88.